GRIT TO TEACH AND THE MINDSET TO STAY: DO YOU HAVE WHAT IT TAKES?

50 Critical Questions to Ask Yourself

by

Paul G. Young, Ph.D.

Terri Green, M.A.

Debra Dunning, Ph.D.

TABLE OF CONTENTS

FOREWORD

Our country will always need a steady stream of highly qualified, energetic, passionate young teachers eager to fill classrooms being vacated by retiring veterans. These individuals will hopefully be among the best and the brightest, from all parts of the nation and all racial, ethnic, political, and socio-economic groups. However, even if they are the best and brightest, statistics show that many will not be fully equipped and prepared for what it takes to survive and thrive during the first challenging years of their career. Even though they'll have acquired the requisite ACT or SAT scores, passed their college courses with good grades, and earned a variety of recognitions and distinctions in related areas, too many will fall flat and quit when they confront the challenges of "real life" in the classroom.

How do we better prepare our teachers and support them during those first years on their own in the classroom? Research clearly shows that the grit factor—the determination to achieve short- and long-term goals, often against difficult odds—coupled with a growth versus a fixed mindset, enables aspiring teachers to develop habits that support their persistence through times of adversity, set-backs, stress, disappointment, and failure. In my book, *Grit to Go*, written with Caleb Grant and Joyce McGreevy, we've developed numerous classroom resources to help teachers motivate growth mindsets in their students. Every classroom teacher should integrate grit and mindset lessons throughout the curriculum.

Grit to Teach and the Mindset to Stay: Do You Have What it Takes? can easily be a companion book to *Grit to Go*, but it is different from other books on the grit or mindset topic because it is packed with important questions, information, ideas, reflection tools, and improvement strategies that will help every aspiring educator better understand the concepts and apply them in personal ways as they develop into a professional. In their college classrooms, the authors analyze 50 important reflective questions, infuse key understandings, stress the importance of deliberate practice, and prepare students to develop the qualities of grit and growth mindset that will set them on a path of perseverance with passion and self-fulfillment that every teacher needs. Forward thinking leaders of teacher preparation programs will replicate these lessons.

While this book centers on the development of college-age aspiring teachers, the key messages and takeaways can be applied to any job, profession, or station in life. This would be a great reading selection for high school students considering career choices. Principals will find it helpful as they assist beginning teachers in sustaining a positive, improvement-focused mindset. The book is packed with good ideas and solid advice for the development of the soft skills needed at any stage of teaching. Reading it will not take up too much of your busy day or the time you must focus on the hard, technical skills you must acquire.

The good news is that grit can be taught and learned. You'll discover something meaningful in this book each time you pick it up, and every time you do, you'll refine your grit skills and better equip yourself for success in the noblest of all professions— teaching.

Jim Grant
Author, Consultant & Founder
Staff Development for Educators,
Peterborough, New Hampshire

INTRODUCTION

So you think you can teach? You might recognize that question as a play on the popular television dance competition with a similar title. The primary allure of reality singing and dancing shows like "So You Think You Can Dance?" "American Idol," and "America's Got Talent," is that new artists are discovered and winners are determined by television viewers. Among other attractions of these shows are the open auditions, where anyone who aspires to sing or dance is welcomed.

Did you ever wonder about the selection process for and time involved in getting those acts staged? Can some people really be that unaware of and unrealistic about their singing or dancing abilities? Why would people allow themselves to be ridiculed and laughed off the stage? Didn't these aspiring performers ask themselves if they really had what it takes to be a star? Didn't they have a coach or a critical friend help them along the way? Did these people seriously envision themselves ready for a performance career?

Several similarities can be loosely drawn between the procedures of auditioning for these shows and aspiring to become a teacher. The processes are generally open at the beginning, but success in any endeavor requires a rigorous development of what are considered hard and soft skills. Preparing for and earning a teaching job encompasses a very selective process. It starts the day you begin to consider whether the career might be for you. The end results are attained when you can deliver a masterful performance on a stage and become a standout in the classroom.

The purpose of this book is to help aspiring teachers make the decision to become a teacher and stick with it. So you think you can teach? Great. Many people do and can. However, as college professors, we are witnessing too many students enter our entry-level teacher education classes at various points in their lives without the awareness, skills, self-discipline, or commitment needed to attain success. If you wonder whether you might lack one or more of these qualities, we hope that rather than wasting your time and money, you will read and study the questions posed in this book and then reflect with your teachers, mentors, peers, loved ones, and others who have understanding and passion for all that is required of educators and decide if teaching is a good fit. Many people should be involved in helping you discern whether you have what it takes to survive and thrive as a teacher. But you must take ownership of the process, ask thoughtful questions, synthesize and evaluate responses, and decide whether or not to commit to the long and continuous growth process. We hope this book provides you with critical discernment questions you might not yet have considered as you ponder and discuss your journey to the classroom.

As scrutiny of college teaching programs continues to rise, so have concerns about who is entering them. Teacher preparation programs across the country often base entry decisions on a range of criteria including GPAs, SAT/ACT scores, interviews, and success on basic skills tests. These are necessary procedural criteria, yet they often fail to identify potential star teachers. From our perspective, we believe that many remedial interventions can be implemented to shore up what an aspiring teacher may not know about curriculum content and pedagogy, and many teacher preparation programs do that well. But beyond that work, we believe many critical questions centered on what are considered "soft skills" of character, work ethic, personal values, core beliefs, and commitment must be addressed. We believe those skills are best evaluated utilizing time-tested, authentic, qualitative assessments and interpersonal observations in college classrooms and school-based apprenticeships. ACT and SAT scores don't adequately predict a teacher's mindset to remain in the classroom. A more reliable indicator is attitude, which often trumps aptitude in predicting long-term success. In fact, many principals tell us they'd rather hire character and train skill.

Our mission as professors is to support students in achieving their goals and to inspire them to stretch toward possibilities they haven't yet considered or thought possible. We are professors, and professors teach, but we are also mentors. We are writing out of fierce concern that students come to us as ready and willing to learn the people skills necessary for effective teaching as they are to master the curriculum and pedagogy of their preferred discipline.

Teachers must be hard workers, skilled thinkers, problem solvers, collaborators, and compassionate, involved citizens. Their future work in classrooms will be socially complex, fiercely competitive, and demanding yet also filled with professional risks, personal fulfillment, and opportunities that span the globe. Our work is to foster our students' unique sense of independence rather than dependence. One important outcome of reading and applying what can be learned from this book is the acquisition of that independence in the form of an artistic ability to express yourself.

Achieving any goal that contains essential and challenging skills requires deliberate practice. Intentional, repetitive practice is imperative for athletes, dancers, musicians, and actors. Teachers are actors on a classroom stage. They must learn from mistakes and from positive and negative experiences and continuously improve their practice. They must possess discipline, desire, commitment, adaptability, and creativity —qualities that are not easy to pinpoint and assess. Those who think with a fixed mindset, who lack the desire to improve, are very much at risk of failing.

Sir Ken Robinson, in his book *Creative Schools*, writes that the fundamental purpose of education is to help students learn.[1] Whether a student is entering preschool or graduating college, that objective is the same. Unfortunately, as Robinson points out, too many distractions cause some teachers to lose focus of what he describes as the heart of education—teachers' relationships with students. For those relationships to be productive and successful, aspiring teachers must develop personal character traits, values, resolve, and skill sets that enable them to react and respond in their own unique way and to persevere through inevitable disruptions in their classrooms, schools, and career advancement. We view the questions in this book as a starting point in the development of closer relationships—with your colleagues, your loved ones, and especially your students.

We want this book foremost to help you understand what it takes to become and stay an effective teacher. We hope you will read it and reflect on important character skills, and that through reflection, you will identify who you are and develop your personal brand. Your intentionality of excellence matters.

Teachers must acquire competence in their area of licensure. That is a minimal expectation. But they must also possess "real world" living dispositions as well as unique curiosities and capacities necessary for

---

1 Robinson, Sir Kenneth (2015). *Creative Schools: The Grassroots Revolution That's Transforming Education*. New York: Penguin/Random House. p. 71

effective teaching. Research has shown that non-cognitive skills such as grit, social sensitivity, optimism, conscientiousness, selflessness, and emotional stability are very important in teacher success.[2] Teachers must prepare intellectually, but they cannot neglect their physical, spiritual, or social maturity. Those capabilities are obviously very personal, but they have implications for teachers' development and well-being, as well as their effectiveness in delivering the curriculum.

The questions posed in this book are designed to help everyone, from potential educators to young professional teachers, identify and cultivate the dispositions and aptitudes that make successful educators, as well as eliminate those that do not. The book should be read by:

- students enrolled in entry-level teacher education classes.
- traditional-aged college students with an undecided major.
- nontraditional-aged college students seeking a career change.
- professors of entry-level teacher education courses and their colleagues.
- members of high school Future Educators Association (FEA) clubs.
- parents of aspiring teachers.
- counselors and career advisors (secondary and post-secondary).
- new teachers.
- school administrators.
- teacher mentors.

We envision the book being used by parents and their children, college students, counselors and advisors, school administrators, and professors as career choices are being pondered and beginning careers are being forged. It can be read and studied in its entirety, by chapters, or by specific, selective questions. Some questions can be singled out for special attention and in-depth study by those seeking personal development and improvement. In no way do we think the questions in this book are all inclusive. These should get you started, help you think and reflect, and lead a quest toward much more that must be addressed for your unique personality, needs, and setting.

---

2   Review the research and writing of Angela Duckworth, Carol Dweck, Paul Tough, and others.

Ultimately, we hope to help aspiring teachers make a career decision that is best for them. If you are considering this field, you should take note that young lives will eventually be impacted by how well you respond to and work through the questions in this book. We hope to help you envision personal and professional success as you prepare to achieve it.

All students deserve teachers who demonstrate grit, possess a growth mindset, and know they have the intangible qualities that lead to success.

Paul Young, Terri Green, and Debra Dunning,
Ohio University-Lancaster
Lancaster, Ohio
May, 2016

CHAPTER 1

PROFESSIONAL ATTITUDE

The following are indicators of professional attitude mindset. How might you rate yourself on each descriptor?

Descriptors	Never	Rarely	Sometimes	Often	Always	Not Sure
1. I focus on the needs of children and youth first.						
2. I have expertise in my content area with a continuous desire to learn.						
3. I willingly work more than a 40-hour workweek.						
4. I do what I say I will do when I say I will do it.						
5. I communicate effectively.						
6. I adhere to the highest values of character and behavior.						
7. I like to praise others.						
8. I am a collaborator and willingly share knowledge.						
9. I say "please" and "thank you."						
10. I always keep a smile on my face.						

These ten indicators of professional attitude are just a beginning. There are, of course, many more. Hopefully, people who know you already recognize that you exhibit these and additional traits every day. A professional attitude is a product of consistent, deliberate practice acquired from years of experience in a classroom. The questions that follow in this chapter and the rest of the book delve into the qualities of a professional attitude in more detail. You'll need a growth mindset and grit to acquire one. Find ways to reflect, discuss, and plan to assure that you always display the qualities of a positive, professional attitude in your own unique way.

Teachers who complain that they are "burned out" have often developed a bad attitude. They'll likely never experience the true meaning of burnout because it is doubtful they ever really caught fire in the first place. (Don't forget to read question 50.)

Question # 1

Do You Have an Attitude?

A bad attitude is like a flat tire. You can't go anywhere until you change it.
—Anonymous

When you walk into a classroom, do you naturally smile? Do you easily make eye contact? Do you carry yourself with confidence, walking erectly with your head up and shoulders back—body language that positions you to communicate effectively? Do you easily display a sense of humor? Do you strive to be courteous and conscientious?

If you and those that know you well can respond positively to those questions, you are well on your way to showing a positive, enthusiastic, welcoming attitude. An honest friend or mentor should be able to help you identify whether you are a source of positive energy or a downer.

Students can quickly perceive teachers with a positive attitude. The obvious indicators are a bright smile, a twinkle of the eye, and consistent upbeat behavioral patterns. Teachers with positive attitudes are friendly to everyone, even those they do not know. They know how to make good first impressions. They strive for excellence. They are decisive, take charge of things in a group, and are the easiest to work with. Their approach to work is motivating. Kids want to be around them, and they enjoy being around kids.

Everyone can improve his or her attitude. Refining your attitude involves improving your mindset. That can be done (and modeled for students) by:

- recognizing when you are down or acting negatively and avoiding ineffective, destructive behaviors.
- accepting who you are and avoiding a comparison of yourself with others.
- being truthful and focused on what makes you most happy.
- acknowledging limits and how much you can juggle without jeopardizing your attitude.

How do you respond to this simple 12-question attitude assessment?

Attitude Indicators	Never	Rarely	Sometimes	Often	Always	Not Sure
1. I smile naturally.						
2. My actions have a purpose of serving a greater good.						
3. I describe my typical days as the same-old, same-old.						
4. I get disappointed when I don't get results I want.						
5. I gravitate to people with a positive attitude.						
6. Friends describe me as possessing a bad attitude.						
7. I wake up early in the day.						
8. I can easily laugh at myself.						
9. I have patience with the limitations of others.						
10. I tend to worry and waste valuable time.						
11. I use labels to describe myself and others.						
12. I express gratitude in a variety of ways.						

There are no correct personal responses, but it is highly recommended that aspiring and new teachers reflect on and discuss these attitude indicators with counselors, teachers, mentors, principals, and others that can guide continuous improvement. Individuals with consistently bad attitudes will never become happy and productive teachers.

Question #2

Do You Have a Sense of Grace and Poise?

We must find time to stop and thank the people who make a difference in our lives.

—John F. Kennedy

Teachers with a sense of grace possess skills and strategies that produce powerful, cordial, and confident conduct in professional and social situations. Those skills include manners, professional etiquette, social kindness, and respect for decorum and protocol.

You must possess common sense to have a sense of grace. It seems that almost daily that the media reports stories about celebrities and public figures (and sometimes educators) who fall from grace, being discredited and losing favor for misguided public or personal behavior. You don't want to become the focus of one of those stories, either as a student or a teacher.

Effective teachers possess a healthy mind, body, and soul. They have the capacity to forgive when they are wronged because they possess abundant love. They bring honor to themselves and others and enhance the profession. They enable their students to realize their potential, acquire dreams, and fulfill them.

As you prepare to become a teacher, work to acquire the social graces—attitude, manners, etiquette, and soft skills (see Question # 3) needed to work with the public. Express feelings of thankfulness and appreciation freely to those who help you achieve your goals. Count your blessings. Show passion for your profession.

Think of a special teacher who demonstrated grace and poise to you and your fellow classmates. Send that teacher a handwritten, personal note, specifying how you observed the skill set, his or her temperament and confidence, and what it meant to you. Writing a letter like this will help you reflect on the traits, as well as identify how to incorporate them into your own classroom. Your act of gratitude will also make that person's day!

Question #3

Can You Talk to People?

The most important single ingredient in the formula of success is knowing how to get along with people.

—Theodore Roosevelt

Sometimes known as the soft skills, your people skills can have as much or more impact on your success in college and your own classroom as your technical teaching skills. Professionals, especially those in a people-oriented business like education, must apply people skills to achieve objectives. While there is no debate that it is extremely important for aspiring teachers to acquire highly developed technical skills for professional success, one of the overarching goals of this book is to stress how it's imperative that you also have great people skills.

Examples of teachers' capacity to effectively utilize people skills are
1. building relationships, knowing students and their families, and doing what is right for them.
2. demonstrating excellent communication skills (oral, written, and non-verbal) and using effective body language.
3. being trustworthy.
4. showing patience and a level head in stressful situations.
5. providing empathetic support, sympathy, and feedback.
6. actively listening without interrupting.
7. displaying genuine concern for other people.
8. showing good judgment with an open mind.
9. proactively solving problems.
10. encouraging and motivating people to do what they didn't think was possible.

Would people who know you well, especially your teachers, indicate that you (a) always, (b) frequently, (c) sometimes, (d) occasionally, or (e) never display these skills and attributes? Reflect with those you trust and respect about how successfully you are able to establish and maintain relationships. How would you respond in an interview if asked for examples of your decision making, responsible behavior, and collaboration?

Effective teachers develop a professional network. They are social. They know how to work in teams and seek feedback about their effectiveness. You must begin to do the same.

Personal attributes, known as people skills, include:
1. A good attitude
2. Sense of humor
3. Honesty
4. Manners and etiquette
5. Empathy
6. Gratitude
7. Initiative
8. Patience
9. Flexibility
10. Self-confidence

CHAPTER 1

DISCUSSION QUESTIONS & PERSONAL GROWTH ACTIVITIES

1. Ask your (friends, teachers, parents) what words they would use to describe you. Create a word cloud that describes you.

2. Have you ever formed a first impression about someone that was obviously inaccurate after you got to know him or her? What qualities or behaviors influenced your first impression?

3. Using a Likert scale (see the Appendix for an example), listen to or watch audio/video recordings identifying nonverbal behaviors that positively and negatively influence first impressions and messaging.

4. Write a thank you note to someone (hopefully a teacher) who exemplified how to make a great first impression, and as a result, made a difference in your life.

5. Watch this YouTube video from the X-Factor television show (see link) and make a list of the many ways "Rachel" displays improper attitude. Discuss your observations with your friends. https://www.youtube.com/watch?v=7S97pcpVeTA

6. Using the survey form below, reflect on the ten soft-skill characteristics listed in Question 3 and throughout this book. Rate yourself and then ask your mentor to discuss your rankings with you and develop strategies for becoming even better. Then, later, complete the survey again. Chart your progress.

Character Attributes	N/A	weakness			average				strength			Comments
		1	2	3	4	5	6	7	8	9	10	
1. Professional Attitude Smile, eye contact, facial expressions, body language, responses, and enthusiasm												
2. Mindset Fixed vs. Growth												
3. Habits Punctuality, responsibility, reliability, honesty, manners, etiquette												
4. Professionalism Attire, actions, thinking												
5. Initiative Willingness to do the extra above and beyond what is required												
6. Reading and Writing Competent habits and skills												
7. Public Speaking Confidence and skills in front of diverse groups												
8. Personal Care Care of mind, body, and soul												
9. Preparation Commitment to learning and practice												
10. Personal Responsibility Insightful questioning vs. complaining, ability to professionally discern												
SUMMARY Add scores from each scene												TOTAL

CHAPTER 1 SELF-ASSESSMENT

HOW TO USE THIS ASSESSMENT GUIDE

Aspiring teachers are nurtured and supported through strong relationships. You should reflect privately, but you should also seek the perspective of and advice from teachers, professors, counselors, parents, friends, and others who can help you discern your personal and professional capacities as you prepare to become a teacher. There are no right answers. Be honest with yourself. When you are finished with this chapter, discuss your self-evaluation (see the chart below) with the people supporting you. Together, your self-evaluation and subsequent discussions should reveal strengths as well as areas for further growth.

If you frequently engage in reflective activities, you should be well prepared for any outcomes of formal evaluation practices.

My preparation and/or professional performance skills indicate that ...	Strongly disagree	Disagree	Neutral	Agree	Strongly agree	No Opinion/ No Response
1. I have a positive attitude.						
2. My mind, body, and soul, including my manners and etiquette, reflect a mature sense of grace.						
3. I have excellent people skills.						

Personal Goal Setting

Smart goals are used by people across the world who choose to develop professionally and personally. Setting clear and achievable goals is a skill. First, you must learn how to define your goal, and before you take any action, to think it through thoroughly. Based on your reflective activities related to any of the chapters, use the outline below to develop individualized improvement and performance goals.

Discernment Question # _____

SMART Goal

Specific Objective (SWBAT)

_____

SWBAT is an acronym for "student will be able to"…
What will you know and be able do as a result of accomplishing this goal?
- What: Identify what you want to accomplish.
- Why: Specific reasons, purpose or benefits of accomplishing the goal.
- Who: Identify who is involved.
- Where: Identify a location.
- Which: Identify requirements and constraints.

Measurable goal (data to collect?)

_____

A measurable goal will usually answer questions such as
- How much?
- How many?
- How will I know when it is accomplished?
- What are the quantifiable indicators that show I've achieved my goal?

Achievable goal (what constitutes success?)

_____

An achievable goal will usually answer the question How?
- How can the goal be accomplished?
- How realistic is the goal based on other constraints?

Realistic

_____

If you have a realistic relevant goal, you can answer yes to these questions:
- Does this seem worthwhile?
- Is this the right time?
- Does this match our other efforts/needs?
- Are you the right person?
- Is it applicable in the current socio-economic environment?

Timely (discuss your envisioned timeline for completing the goal)

_____

A time-bound goal will usually answer the question
- When?
- What can I do six months from now?
- What can I do six weeks from now?
- What can I do today?

CHAPTER 2

MINDSET

How would people who know you best, especially your teachers, describe your mindset? Would they say things like the following about you?

"She often complains that assignments are too hard."

"He thinks his work is good enough."

"She doesn't like to hear what I have to say about her work."

"He's smart, but he never applies himself."

"She gives up way too easily and quickly."

If teachers have said such things about you, they are implying that you have fixed mindset tendencies. Those characteristics will limit your ability to develop effective relationships with students, properly address routine challenges, and achieve personal satisfaction as a teacher. Bear in mind, people have a combination of both fixed and growth mindsets. However, this book is about developing a growth mindset.

The questions in this chapter are intended to help you distinguish the indicators of growth mindset and grit, qualities that every effective teacher must possess. Find multiple ways to reflect, discuss, and plan to assure that you always display qualities of grit and growth mindset in your own, unique way.

Question # 4

Do You Have a Fixed or Growth Mindset?

Don't tell me how talented you are. Tell me how hard you work.
—Arthur Rubenstein, classical pianist

Have you ever had a teacher who thought you or your classmates were not good students and treated you accordingly? That teacher likely had a fixed mindset. Teachers with fixed mindsets assume that intelligence and talent are fixed at birth and they can do little to help their students succeed at higher levels.

Stanford Professor Carol Dweck's research about mindset is being used all over the world to counter the assumption that intelligence is fixed at birth.[3] Her research demonstrates how intelligence is malleable. With encouragement, good training, and a willing attitude, students of all ages and backgrounds can expand their ability to learn. Yet, many practices and actions in K–12 schools and college classrooms continue to reflect, and often reinforce, a fixed mindset philosophy.

Aspiring teachers must become knowledgeable about the importance of mindset philosophy for two reasons:

1. The tendencies of your personal mindset (growth vs. fixed) will influence your college classroom performance and ultimate productivity in a classroom.
2. Your ability to teach students how to acquire growth mindset abilities and personalities will be limited if you fail to understand or internalize the tenets of the theory in your own behaviors and way of thinking.

---

3   Dweck, Carol (2006). *Mindset: The New Psychology of Success.* New York: Random House.

Dweck's work is summarized in Table 1. As you review it, reflect on the questions:

	Strongly disagree	Disagree	Neutral	Agree	Strongly agree	No Opinion/ No Response
1. If a math concept is difficult, do you choose not to figure it out because you've been told you were not good at math?						
2. If a teacher suggests that you study more for tests, do you follow the suggestion?						
3. If a major class project is due on Monday, do you buckle down and do it or allow distractions and other interests to get in the way of completion?						

Did your responses to the questions reflect more of a fixed or a growth mindset? How do you think your teachers (or a supervising teacher or a boss) would view your typical classroom performance through the mindset filter?

Closely related to Dweck's work are the ideas of Paul Tough, explained in his book, *How Children Succeed: Grit, Curiosity, and the Hidden Power of Character* (2012, Houghton Mifflin Harcourt). Tough argues that the qualities that matter most in developing a growth mindset philosophy are related to character skills like perseverance, curiosity, conscientiousness, optimism, and self-control (see question # 5).

Applying what you learn about mindset can transform your performance as a student and your success as a teacher. You'll discover ways in which parents do—and do not—prepare their children for adulthood. You'll learn strategies to improve the lives of children growing up in poverty. Discussing mindset should inspire you and your peers to better understand how you teach life skills that make school a better experience for all kids.

TABLE 1

	Fixed Mindset (student has a desire to appear smart but just get by)	Growth Mindset (student has a desire to learn and grow)
Challenges	*Avoids them*	*Embraces them*
Obstacles	*Gives up easily*	*Persists with grit*
Effort	*Sees it as fruitless*	*Sees it as the path to mastery*
Criticism	*Ignores it, even if useful*	*Learns from it*
Success of Others	*Feels threatened by it*	*Becomes inspired by it*

From the work of Carol S. Dweck
Mindset: The New Psychology of Success, 2006

References and Reading Recommendations

Dweck, Carol (2007). *Mindset: The New Psychology of Success.* New York, NY: Random House.

Ricci, Mary (2013). *Mindsets in the Classroom: Building a Culture of Success and Student Achievement in Schools.* Waco, TX: Prufrock Press, Inc.

Tough, Paul (2012). *How Children Succeed: Grit, Curiosity, and the Hidden Power of Character.* Boston: Houghton Mifflin Harcourt.

Principals know that if they ask kindergarteners to sing, dance, or reach for the ceiling, they'll try without much hesitation. But if they ask middle schoolers to do the same, they'll likely put their heads down to avoid eye contact, interaction, and acknowledgement of their peers. It seems that the confidence and persistence of too many students is beaten out of them during elementary school.

It is imperative that rather than sequestering innate talents and abilities, teachers learn how to instill curiosity, initiative, and persistence in their students to help them grow.

Question # 5

Do You Know What Grit Is?

Grit is living life like it's a marathon, not a sprint.

—Angela Lee Duckworth

How would you respond to these twelve statements?
1. I have overcome setbacks in my life to achieve goals.
2. New ideas and projects distract me and keep me from finishing work.
3. I have changing interests.
4. I don't easily get discouraged by setbacks.
5. After a short time with an idea or project, I lose interest.
6. I am a hard worker.
7. I often set a goal but then later pursue another one.
8. If projects take too long to complete, I lose interest and focus.
9. I finish whatever I begin.
10. I have achieved a goal that took several years to complete.
11. I become interested in new pursuits every few months.
12. I am diligent.

There are no right or wrong answers. The statements, slightly modified and without multiple choice answers, align with a twelve-item grit scale developed by Angela Duckworth and associates at the University of Pennsylvania. [4] Grit is a personality trait, defined by Duckworth as "perseverance and passion for long-term goals, that some people have more of than others." Her ongoing research is exploring whether grit may be a key to college success.

He's smart, but he just needs to apply himself. Has anyone ever said that about you or some of your friends? Would people describe you, based on your observable behavioral patterns, as someone who easily gives up, or are you the student in a complex, challenging class that never gives up?

---

4   Duckworth, A.L., Peterson, C., Matthews, M.D., & Kelly, D.R. (2007). Grit: Perseverance and passion for long-term goals. Journal of Personality and Social Psychology, 9, 1087-1101. Duckworth, A. (2016). *Grit: The Power of Passion and Perseverance.* New York: Scribner.

Grit is an essential character skill for the workplace. It is embodied in a "can do" attitude, and Duckworth's research shows that a gritty attitude often trumps aptitude. Grit is a component of common work ethic skills. It can be taught and reinforced in the school, home, and community. Grit will become part of the 2017 National Assessment of Educational Progress (NAEP) testing program, with the goal to provide a critical window into how students' motivation, mindset, and grit can affect their learning. [5]

In our instant-gratification, short-attention-span, multitasking world, many have lost sight of persistence as a core element of high achievement. Teachers need grit themselves, and they must be able to teach it to their students. College students preparing to become teachers need the grit to persevere through the challenges of balancing coursework, family, work, and other obligations.

So, if you're thinking you aren't very gritty, research this topic. Speak with your teachers and counselors and develop a 6-step plan (building upon the work of Thomas Hoerr) for how they or a mentor can assist you. [6]

1. Establish a supportive environment where you can work through a challenging project.
2. Set clear expectations about how to achieve goals.
3. Learn grit vocabulary and teach it to others.
4. Experience frustration and explain how you felt dealing with it.
5. Monitor the experience.
6. Reflect on what you learned and plan for improvement.

> The construct of grit dates back to the work of Sir Francis Galton (*Hereditary Genius*, 1869) and the tenacity has been considered a virtue since the time of Aristotle.

5   Sparks, S. 'Nation's Report Card' to Gather Data on Grit, Mindset. Education Week, June 6, 2015.
6   *Fostering Grit: How Do I Prepare My Students for The Real World?* Alexandria, VA: ASCD.

Link to 12-Item Grit Scale, Duckworth Lab, University of Pennsylvania
https://upenn.app.box.com/s/et30heyb2e7keq4t2w8b7c65l230pscn

Despite spending hours researching and planning what they think will be a wonderful lesson, teachers sometimes experience failure. Those who can accept failure, learn from it, and keep coming back with different ideas and strategies demonstrate grit. The learning that occurs from good failure, both for the students and the teacher, leads to meaningful and memorable outcomes upon which greater obstacles can be ameliorated.

Question # 6

Are You Envious of Others?

The most difficult instrument to play in the orchestra is second fiddle.
—Leonard Bernstein

Those who have participated in a musical ensemble or a team sport can likely recall times of feeling envy. Only one quarterback calls plays and one trumpet player plays solos. There are back-up players in the second chair or the second team. They do the same preparation work but seldom get to play a lead part. Those with the fixed mindset often get discouraged and quit. Only those possessing a gritty growth mindset and dedication stick with the program.

Do you become envious of classmates who perform better, win awards, and receive recognition? It's nearly impossible to sidestep because envy is an unavoidable consequence of the comparisons we seem programmed to make. Left unchecked, envy can become an ugly, vicious emotion. Malicious envy stifles growth and innovation. But as students mature, demonstrate progress, and move through teacher preparation programs, those with a true growth mindset develop a benign form of envy that's tinged with admiration rather than resentment.

Music and athletic programs promote numerous cliché statements that you likely know, such as "There is no 'I' in team," "Good things happen to people that wait," or "Be who you are." When you become a teacher, you are part of an entire staff, not a soloist. You can and will lead, but your success will be greater as part of the team.

But wait! To become part of a school staff, you and your classmates might compete for the same jobs. If you aren't the selected candidate, you may once again feel you can never escape the conditions of playing from second chair. Constant competition may make you feel you have only a handful of true friends, so treat them well. Show them gratitude. Doing so will support your attitude, which will boost others' perception of your aptitude.

So, what can you do if you see yourself constantly as part of the second team?

First, show grit regardless of your self-perceived ranking. Make sure you are making every effort to continuously improve through deliberate practice. Be certain that others notice your contributions regardless of the chair or team you are assigned. You will be selected for the job where your skills best compliment the team. You have unique strengths.

Second, realize that what appear to be important comparisons now likely won't matter in five years. Don't let envy ruin your relationships and erode the 'team' culture. Never allow your desire to be the star of the show diminish your enjoyment of being part of it. Imagine the role of a triangle player in an orchestra—often overlooked until the music requires the performer to contribute with special technique and skills.

Lastly, don't ever allow yourself to become an arrogant first-chair player. Don't flaunt your success. If feelings related to envy continue to bother you, talk them out with your mentor, teachers, coaches, or counselors. If you allow these feelings to fester, you'll never overcome them.

Question # 7

Are You Good at Analyzing?

If someone asks how you did after you complete an important paper or class presentation, do you typically respond with something vague, like, "I think I did well," or is your answer much more reflective and self-critical?

Often, student responses resemble the former more than the latter—because analytical skills require years of development. Analysis is the process of breaking complex concepts into smaller parts in order to gain a better understanding of them. Students must be taught to study, examine, scrutinize, investigate, and evaluate as part of the development of the analytic processes. Teachers guide this development by asking questions that lead to higher-order thinking.

Dr. Benjamin Bloom published a handbook in 1956, known today as Bloom's Taxonomy, that distinguishes fundamental questions that teachers should ask to increase students' knowledge and skills at six levels (see Table 2). His work has become a foundational element in teaching.

To ask students about their papers or presentations with an intentional desire to expand analytic thinking, teacher's questions should include key words and statements such as:

1. How/what would you compare this work to…?
2. Can you differentiate/distinguish between…?
3. What evidence do you have to…?
4. What ways can you demonstrate progress from…?
5. Why do you think…?

When teachers ask questions that drive analytic thinking, students learn to cite better evidence of their thinking, compare and contrast, and support generalizations with facts.

Teachers must be able to analyze many kinds of complex situations involving people, particularly their students, on multiple levels. They must demonstrate an ability to apply logical thinking when gathering and analyzing information about student performance. They must design and test solutions to problems and formulate effective, creative plans of action. Merging scientific analysis with gut reactions (intuition) to make good decisions is a daily part of teaching.

So what can aspiring teachers do to improve their ability to analyze?

1. Reflect and discuss your problem-solving skills with a trusted friend or mentor.
2. Determine if your analytical processes and decisions are more influenced by logic or intuition.
3. Look for inconsistencies in your decision-making processes related to people, practices, performance, and professionalism.
4. Focus your attention where it is needed most—analyzing how prepared you are to become an educator, your relationships, networking skills, good and bad habits, and overall level of curiosity.

TABLE 2

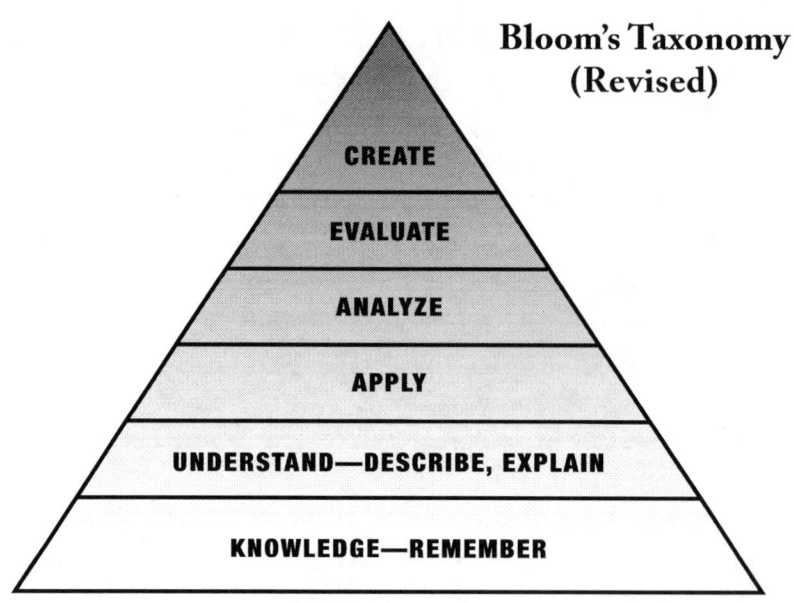

Bloom's Taxonomy (Revised)

CREATE

EVALUATE

ANALYZE

APPLY

UNDERSTAND—DESCRIBE, EXPLAIN

KNOWLEDGE—REMEMBER

Based on an APA adaption of Anderson, L.W. & Krathwohl, D.R. (Eds.) (2001)

Recommended Web Resources:

1. http://edglossary.org/blooms-taxonomy/
2. http://www.learningandteaching.info/learning/bloomtax.htm
3. http://teaching.uncc.edu/learning-resources/articles-books/best-practice/goals-objectives/blooms-educational-objectives

Question # 8

Can You Commit to Teaching?

Commitment to teaching means...
- working hard, every day (and many weekends), all year.
- reading and grading papers after work hours.
- writing detailed daily lesson plans for multiple classes.
- showing up to work even when you don't feel well.
- willingly reaching deep into your own pocket to provide financial assistance to help those in need.
- living the example you want your students to become.

Commitment means feeling dedication and loyalty to a cause, activity, or profession. You should develop a level and type of commitment that is unique to you. To commit to teaching means you are willing to be put in charge and have the welfare of students entrusted to you. An obligation to students' wellbeing may at times restrict your personal freedom of action.

Making a commitment to teaching must be grounded in reality. You must understand that it is an agreement to do something in the future. Commitment is different from a contract, which is a legally binding exchange of promises.

Commitment is professional action without excuses. Committed teachers don't whine about how hard things are or put their concern about what others might think before their concern for their students. Nothing gets in their way of doing what is best for students.

Another way of approaching commitment is to "do what you say you will do when you say you will do it."

Question # 9

Are You Mobile?

After college, where do you hope to live and work? Do you have commitments that require you to remain in a certain geographic area? If you do, you should research the job market for teachers in your area. If the job market in your desired area is saturated, you may not want to spend time and money earning a degree and a teaching license. However, if you are mobile and willing to relocate, you will find there are shortages in various parts of the country.

Review the needs and hiring practices of schools in your preferred work area. Acquire the licensure and certifications that make you most employable. Make yourself known to future employers/references within that radius, especially the key influence makers (kingpins).

When seeking employment, don't send applications to schools or districts where you would never accept a position. It is a waste of both your time and the time of the interviewers.

Mobility could also become an issue once you begin your teaching career. If you end up moving from job to job each year, you should be prepared to explain why. Interviewers will wonder and want to know why. It is wise to address justifiable reasons in your resume and cover letter.

School administrators devote many hours to the teacher recruitment and selection process. When a candidate is selected, they prefer a multi-year commitment because this benefits students. An unexplained record of mobility might imply negative issues about a teacher's employment record.

CHAPTER 2

DISCUSSION QUESTIONS & PERSONAL GROWTH ACTIVITIES

1. Share a personal grit story. Why do you think this question might be asked during an interview? What insights about your character and work ethic does your grit story unveil? Start analyzing the personal grit stories of others.

2. Utilize grit vocabulary words and give real world examples that exemplify each one in ways that the students you will teach will understand.

3. List at least five (5) ways in which you can show commitment in a learning environment.

    a)

    b)

    c)

    d)

    e)

4. Take the 12 questions GRIT Survey by Duckworth. (http://www.sas.upenn.edu/~duckwort/images/12-item%20Grit%20Scale.05312011.pdf)

5. Determine if you have a tendency toward a fixed or growth mindset using Carol Dweck's online tool: http://www. mindsetonline.com/testyourmindset/step1.php

6. Read Thomas Hoerr's ASCD Aria *Fostering Grit: How Do I Prepare My Students for the Real World?*

7. Review one of the recommended websites at the end of question 7 and discuss it with a mentor.

8. Observe the Chris Gardner interview clip in *The Pursuit of Happyness* (Alper, Clayman, D'Esposito, Zee, 7 Muccino, 2006: see http://www.youtube.com/watch?v=gHXKitKAT1E) and discuss examples of fixed and growth mindset including both non-verbal actions and verbal comments.

CHAPTER 2 SELF-ASSESSMENT

HOW TO USE THIS ASSESSMENT GUIDE

Aspiring teachers are nurtured and supported through strong relationships. You should reflect privately, but you should also seek the perspective of and advice from teachers, professors, counselors, parents, friends, and others who can help you discern your personal and professional capacities as you prepare to become a teacher. There are no right answers. Be honest with yourself. When you are finished with this chapter, discuss your self-evaluation (see the chart below) with the people supporting you. Together, your self-evaluation and subsequent discussions should reveal strengths as well as areas for further growth.

If you frequently engage in reflective activities, you should be well prepared for any outcomes of formal evaluation practices.

My preparation and/or professional performance skills indicate that ...	Strongly disagree	Disagree	Neutral	Agree	Strongly agree	No Opinion/ No Response
4. I can demonstrate specific indicators of a growth mindset.						
5. I am not jealous of the success of my peers and colleagues.						
3. I regularly exhibit characteristics of perseverance, resilience, and grit.						
7. My analytical skills are well developed.						

8. I am committed to becoming a teacher.						
9. I am free to teach in any geographic location.						

CHAPTER 3

HABITS

All our life ... is but a mass of habits.

—William James
19th-century Psychologist

Charles Duhigg, in his book *The Power of Habit: Why We Do What We Do in Life and Business*, describes the development of habits as a three-part process:

1. Identification of a cue (a trigger for an automatic behavior to begin).
2. Recognition of a routine (the desired behavior of habit).
3. Attainment of a reward (something worth repeating).

To cite examples, Duhigg explains how to change a fingernail biting habit or avoid eating cookies. Studies show that the urge to bite a nail (or to eat a cookie) begins with a feeling of tension. To change behavior, one must learn a competing response (e.g., placing hands in pockets, holding or gripping something, ensuring quick access to a better food choice to put in the mouth—anything that encourages a better physical response). The reward is an intrinsic feeling of accomplish, happiness, and physical improvement (e.g., improved fingernail hygiene or weight loss). Cues and rewards don't change, but routine behaviors do.

Duhigg's work provides an effective template for an aspiring teacher who wants to change from fixed mindset behavior patterns to the more desirable and productive attributes of a growth mindset. Only with a strong sense of grit, a commitment to carry on and achieve a sometimes-challenging goal, can habits be changed.

The questions that follow in this chapter are intended to provide insights and initiate discussion about the growth mindset behaviors needed to shape positive habits, and perhaps change negative ones. Find multiple ways to reflect, discuss, and plan to assure that you always display good, professional habits in your own unique way.

Question # 10

Do You Have Charisma?

Charisma. You can't buy it, you can't make it. And you sure can't fake it.

—unknown

The Oxford English Dictionary defines *charisma* as "compelling attractiveness or charm that can inspire devotion in others." [7] Fortunately, it's a behavioral quality that anyone can develop. It's useful in the classroom or anywhere a teacher is engaged in actions of leading, coaching, selling, speaking, mentoring, and developing positive relationships with diverse groups of people.

From the moment you meet them, even if you know nothing about them, charismatic teachers come across as unique, maybe even a little bit weird, but impressive nonetheless. As you contemplate becoming a teacher, consider how your friends, and especially the former teachers you admire, would describe you. Would they say you were charismatic? Do you exhibit vitality and abundance of life? Do you manage your body language and appearance well? When you walk into a room, do people notice? Do you speak with clarity, choosing words that make a huge impact? Do you smile and show a sense of humor? Do you have an awareness of emotions and the ability to manage moods? Do you exhibit empathy for others by listening gently?

If you are a young aspiring teacher, you may never have needed to consider your charismatic appeal. But you can't wait until your field placements, student teaching, or job interviews to begin developing it. Typically, skills related to charisma are not intentionally taught in college, but they are a learnable, highly desirable set of habits and abilities.

---

7   http://www.oxforddictionaries.com/definition/english/charisma

Tips for Developing Charisma

1. Maintain a healthy diet and body weight. Get plenty of exercise. Develop regular sleep habits. Make time for yourself. Balance your professional and personal life.

2. Stand up straight, keep shoulders back, and carry yourself with dignity.

3. Become aware of your feelings (it's okay to have a bad day, everyone does) and stay focused and sensitive when listening to others. Treat people as you want them to treat you.

4. Analyze what shapes your self-esteem and develop these emotions. Smile. Laugh. Act accordingly to your core values.

5. Increase your confidence by acting despite your fear. Take advantage of opportunities to speak in public, sing, dance, act, and ask questions in every class you take or professional development training you attend.

6. Learn to relax under pressure. (We strongly recommend acting and improvisation classes.)

7. Practice speaking with clarity and conviction. Record your voice. Singing lessons, acting, and breathing work will help improve your vocal quality. Correct grammar is an essential skill for teachers. Learn to self-correct any improper grammatical or colloquial sayings you have (e.g., dropping the *ing* and saying words like *stoppin'* instead of *stopping*) immediately.

8. Create time for yourself. Listen to soothing music, meditate, pray, or engage in any aspirations that help train your attention to your inner needs.

9. Be honest and bold, but don't offend people. Behave as an equal to others. Each person's charisma may manifest slightly differently. You want to be charismatic in order to appeal to the students you'll teach.

10. Never lose sight of what drives you to become a teacher—the kids. Remind yourself of this daily. Visuals might include quotes or photos for your study area.

Question # 11

Are You a Role Model?

Children have more need of models than of critics.
— Carolyn Coats, Author
Things Your Mother Always Told You, But You Didn't Want to Hear

Throughout the history of American education, teachers have been held to the highest standard, expected to live decent, productive lives in a democratic society. As role models, they wield tremendous influence. They must lead effectively and clearly communicate expectations to students. They must engage continuously in reflection upon their actions, encourage teamwork and cooperation, and support others in their growth and development. Teacher role models demonstrate confidence in themselves.

What does the standard for being a role model look like?
Teacher/role models must consistently…
- display kindness.
- be encouraging.
- follow the rules of etiquette and display good manners.
- make good choices.
- show generosity.
- share with others.
- honor commitments.
- develop appropriate, productive relationships.

What can a preservice teacher do to gain recognition as a role model?
- Show passion for your learning/work. Passion is infectious.
- Live your values.
- Become active in your community/school/work.
- Develop skills and abilities needed to overcome obstacles.
- Become a hero to someone (such as a relative, neighbor, or student). Go out of your way to help someone in need or act in ways that inspire others.
- Never lose sight of where you came from and how you got where you are.
- Share your story to help/inspire others.

One morning, the father of a third-grade boy came to school and asked to see the teacher who "walks on water." "What are you talking about?" the principal asked. So again, the parent said, "I want to see this teacher you have here who walks on water. My son has been coming home since the start of the school year telling me and my wife that his teacher does this, that, and everything under the sun. He sings, he dances, he reads compelling stories and gets my son to behave and respond in the class in ways we've surely never seen at home. The way my son talks about him, I'm sure this teacher must be able to 'walk on water'."

What a compliment. The teacher the parent wanted to meet and observe was a second-year teacher, responsible for a split second-third grade class. He was equipped with a positive attitude and a growth mindset and possessed charm and personality traits way beyond his age and years of experience. His influence as a role model for kids became legendary in that school.

Question # 12

What's Your Excuse?

Don't do what you'll have to find an excuse for.

—Proverb

An excuse a day will keep your goals at bay.

—Paul Young

Any teacher can likely recall dozens of excuses from their students about how their dog ate a backpack full of homework. Those same dogs apparently like college homework, too.

Millennials have been characterized for their use of the response, "Yeah, but." Excuse makers are often procrastinators. They don't understand priorities and are quick to place blame on others. They don't take care of themselves and frequently complain that they are tired. If they are depressed or ill, they should certainly take care of themselves and see a physician. But they should not cry wolf if nothing is really wrong.

Effective teachers acknowledge problems, face the facts, and react to challenges and difficulties with a growth mindset (see Question # 4). They learn to avoid dwelling on problems. Instead, they create solutions. They avoid rationalizations, admitting when they are wrong or neglectful. They also don't allow others to take advantage of them.

If you have a tendency to complain, work on stopping this behavior. We know your dog didn't really eat your homework! Learn from your mistakes and those of others. Don't make or accept excuses.

References
Coats, C. (1994). *Things Your Mother Always Told You but You Didn't Want to Hear.* Nashville: Thomas Nelson Publishers.

CHAPTER 3

DISCUSSION QUESTIONS AND PERSONAL GROWTH ACTIVITIES

1. Make a list of some personal habits you observe in others that you like and don't like. Share these and discuss them with your classmates and friends. After the discussion, make a list of your personal habits that you are proud of, as well as those you would like to break.

2. Share one of your favorite quotes. After sharing this quote with others, begin collecting inspirational quotes that motivate and inspire you.

3. Identify a problem you are currently experiencing, and list some possible solutions.

4. Make a recording of yourself describing something that you are passionate about. Analyze your strengths and weaknesses. What is your "gut reaction" as you watch yourself?

5. To begin understanding the power of YET, practice replacing the phrase "I can't" in your vocabulary with the phrase "I can't *yet*."

6. Keep a list of the excuses you hear from others or you say to yourself in the course of a day or a week. Identify them as indicators of a fixed or growth mindset.

CHAPTER 3 SELF-ASSESSMENT

Aspiring teachers are nurtured and supported through strong relationships. You should reflect privately, but you should also seek the perspective of and advice from teachers, professors, counselors, parents, friends, and others who can help you discern your personal and professional capacities as you prepare to become a teacher. There are no right answers. Be honest with yourself. When you are finished with this chapter, discuss your self-evaluation (see the chart below) with the people supporting you. Together, your self-evaluation and subsequent discussions should reveal strengths as well as areas for further growth.

If you frequently engage in reflective activities, you should be well prepared for any outcomes of formal evaluation practices.

My preparation and/or professional performance skills indicate that …	Strongly disagree	Disagree	Neutral	Agree	Strongly agree	No Opinion/ No Response
10. I radiate vitality, charm, and personality in social and professional settings.						
11. I am a positive role model among my friends and peers.						
12. I do not make excuses for my shortcomings.						

CHAPTER 4

PROFESSIONALISM

What is professionalism? Consider the following attributes:
1. Adherence to cultural norms in a school and community.
2. Friendly, respectful relations with all kinds of people.
3. Conscientious attitude toward work.
4. Self-responsibility and ownership of behavior.
5. Acceptance of feedback (positive and negative).
6. Impeccable communications (oral and written).
7. Flexibility.
8. Reliability (rarely or never being late or forgetting commitments).
9. Initiative (doing more than what is minimally required).
10. Cooperative collaboration (a team player).

A century ago, society seemed to hold teachers and the education profession in general in higher esteem than perhaps is the case today. Then, teachers were ranked as among the most educated members of their communities. Times have changed. Lack of respect for individual teachers and society's irreverence of the profession has increased as adherence to professional standards have deteriorated.

You and your peers can reverse those trends if you adopt growth mindset qualities of professionalism. We are counting on you.

The questions in this chapter are intended to help you understand several key indicators of professional qualities that every effective teacher must possess. These questions are an introduction to fully understanding the concept of professionalism. Find multiple ways to reflect, discuss, and plan to assure that you develop high levels of professionalism in your own unique way.

Question #13

Can You Pass a Background Check?
Do You Have Any Secrets?

Social media is changing the way we communicate and the way we are perceived, both positively and negatively. Every time you post a photo or update your status, you are contributing to your own digital footprint and personal brand.

—Amy Jo Martin
American Author

Did you know that as a prospective teacher, you must go through a background check?[8] Schools carry out these checks to ensure students' safety. This procedure is legally mandated in all fifty states in the U.S. [9]

Initially, you will be fingerprinted so that a government agency such as the Federal Bureau of Investigation (FBI) and/or Bureau of Criminal Investigation (BCI) can determine if you have a criminal background. This process is only the beginning. There are additional teacher background checks that are likely completed. These include, but are not limited to, checking driving records, past employment records, educational certification, current and previous addresses, credit history, court records, and bankruptcies. Your social media digital footprint will also be one of the first items to be checked and evaluated for improper behavior.

There are many ways to ensure that you pass a background check. Make sure there are no discrepancies between any of your professional documents, including your application, references, resume and what is reported by schools and others in prior work experiences. The personal and professional data that you report on these documents must be accurate and factual. Incorrect reporting, or the withholding of deep, dark secrets is usually discovered, so make sure to always be honest and upfront with future employers. Past problems, especially if they occurred a long time ago, may not have any bearing on the present. However, most school districts have a "zero-tolerance" policy when it comes to a criminal history.

---

8   http://education.ohio.gov/Topics/Teaching/Educator-Licensure/Additional-Information/Background-Check-FAQs
9   https://www.teach.org/teaching-certification

Always read and answer questions accurately and fully. Conduct a self-background check by viewing your web footprints. Look at what you have said and what others have said about you. Do a Google search of your name and read social media postings. If, for some explainable reason, small red flags do appear but should not impact your ability to teach, see if those citations can be expunged. Make sure to contact the individuals you are using as references so they can be prepared with their responses. Honesty is always the best policy, especially in the teaching profession.

What follows are some questions you can ask yourself as you prepare to pass your background checks:

1. Have I made my social media accounts private?
2. Did I look at my web footprints and remain satisfied with what was found?
3. Do I honor the "ten-mile rule" by not frequenting bars/clubs in my community?
4. Is my FBI/BCI record clean?
5. Do I keep my private relationships (AKA personal life) private?
6. Do I listen to the little voice in my head that says, "If I can't tell my parents, then I probably shouldn't do it?"
7. Do I make sure never to drink or text and drive?
8. Do I avoid social events where inappropriate or illegal behavior is taking place?
9. Do I avoid people who make unprofessional choices and say unprofessional things?
10. Would a parent accept me as a role model for his or her child?

Remember, in this digital age, data mining is easy. Cameras and information are everywhere. If it's on the web, it will likely be retrievable, forever. Your actions reflect positively or negatively now and cast shadows on your future. Teachers are held to a higher standard than many other professionals.

Are you sure you still want to be a teacher?

Many problems originating from college parties where underage drinking and the use of unlawful drugs are prevalent can later resurface to haunt teacher candidates. All actions have ramifications. Make good choices. Think beyond what is happening in real time.

To learn more about how schools conduct background checks, follow these links.

https://www.youtube.com/watch?v=njhLEcdzSKg&feature=player_embedded

http://education.ohio.gov/Topics/Teaching/Educator-Licensure/Additional-Information/Background-Check-FAQs

https://www.teach.org/teaching-certification

Question # 14

Are Your Tattoos and Piercings Worth Coming in Second Place?

My body is my journal, and my tattoos are my story.

—Johnny Depp

Appearance is important in a professional setting. If you have a tattoo or a body piercing, you may wonder if they are appropriate in the workplace or will impact your ability to get a job. Principals express varying opinions about hiring teachers with visible tattoos. Facial piercings (lip, brow, nose, and tongue) are generally viewed as inappropriate in the teaching profession and inconsistent with professional standards of decorum. Tattoos may raise questions or send offensive messages. There are differing opinions on what is acceptable. Perhaps the most important question to ask, especially for young students and their parents, is, "Is any body art worth positioning yourself to potentially be considered in second or third place compared to other candidates?"

> While many older professionals responsible for hiring remain uncomfortable with body art and view it as unprofessional, numerous young people are choosing to tattoo and pierce. According to the American College of Emergency Physicians, as of December 2011, 36 percent of Americans ages 25–29 had at least, one tattoo and 47 percent of Americans ages 16–20 had at least one body piercing other than the earlobe.

If you have a tattoo or a piercing, you may be thinking that you are protected by your First Amendment rights to freedom of expression. However, this is not true. Employers can limit personal expression on the job as long as they do not impinge on employees' civil liberties. According to the Equal Employment Opportunity Commission (EEOC), employers are allowed to impose dress codes and appearance policies as long as they do not discriminate based on or hinder a person's race, color, religion, age, national origin, or gender. Many school districts have some kind of dress code or concealment policy.

So, think before you pierce and ink. Ask yourself these questions:

1. Do I know the culture of the school?
2. Is there a school policy on concealment of tattoos and piercings?
3. Is there a student/teacher dress code?
4. Is my desire to have a tattoo or piercing cosmetic, a fashion statement, or does it hold a much deeper significance?
5. Will the administrator hiring me be a member of the older generation that, for the most part, believes tattoos and piercings are unprofessional?
6. Will tattoos and piercings be popular twenty years from now?
7. Why is there a market for tattoo removal creams and tattoo removal options?
8. Is it better to be conservative and remove my piercings and cover my tattoos and err on the side of caution when I enter the school?
9. Is it worth the risk of potentially limiting my marketability and employment opportunities in a tight job market to pierce and tattoo?
10. As a role model, will I be sending my desired message to my students?

Finally, realize that as a future teacher, your personal decisions, actions, and uniqueness must be reconciled with professional standards and expectations. Teachers' actions are always a subject of discussion, negotiation, and compromise.

To learn more about how principals view tattoos, follow the links to these websites.
https://www.youtube.com/watch?v=Ky7OBHkOx4Y
http://www.eeoc.gov/

Question # 15

Do You Know How to Dress Like a Teacher?

Dress first class, think first class, act first class.
—Dr. Samuel Sava, former Executive Director
National Association of Elementary School Principals (NAESP)

What do you see when you look in the mirror? Do you look like a teacher? Do you see someone who looks well-groomed and confident? Do your clothes look comfortable yet business-like? Do you look like someone professional colleagues would want to work with, parents would trust, and students would respect?

First impressions matter. You have approximately five seconds to be perceived positively or negatively by others. Many times a person's perception of you is based on how you look. "Dress for success" should be your motto. Your attire speaks to who you are as a person and as a professional. It is difficult to overcome a poor first impression, and as a result, how you dress is an important part of your credibility. Colleagues, administrators, students, and parents will be evaluating your professionalism and your potential performance as a teacher.

So, what is professional and appropriate? It is essential that you showcase your best on-the-job look. Let's start at the top, going from head to toe. Only natural hair colors work here—no blue, pink, or purple hair. Hair should be neat and clean, including men's facial hair. Many professional women wear make-up as long as it is not overdone. Pierced earrings are appropriate as long as they are not too distracting. Other piercings on the nose, brow, and lips should be removed unless approved by the principal. If possible, tattoos should be covered. Clothes should be loose fitting and well-tailored, with a nice shape and style so that they are comfortable to wear. Skirts, dresses, pants, and yes, even maxi-dresses are good choices. Women should not wear mini-skirts, see-through clothing, yoga pants, spandex, or anything low-cut. Men should not wear shorts or t-shirts. Trousers and shirts with button-down collars (and a tie) are great choices. Both men and women should avoid sweatpants or sweatshirts unless they are physical education teachers. Jeans should be worn only on dress-down days. Comfortable shoes are a must, but not flip-flops, crocs, tennis shoes, or sandals. Women should not wear shoes with extremely high heels.

Your clothes should reflect your personality and your personal brand. Dressing too casually gives off an undisciplined vibe that might undermine your ability to teach with respect and authority. But dressing too rigidly could have the opposite effect, creating a sense of separation between you and your students. Be aware of the products you buy. Think about the perfumes/colognes you use, the jewelry you wear, and the styles of clothing you select. You are sending a message wherever you go. You are messaging your personality.

It also might be a good time to reorganize your closet. Your professional wardrobe should not include t-shirts with inappropriate messages, t-shirts intended to be underwear, tank tops, or spaghetti strap tops. In addition to the clothing items also mentioned, your professional wardrobe should not include sheer tops, low cut tops, shorts, mini-skirts, skirts with front slits, flip flops, sandals, athletic performance shoes/sneakers, torn clothes or clothes with holes, sweatshirts or hoodies, cargo pants, or spandex.

When you need to dress professionally, for an interview, a student teaching position, or a new job as a teacher, a quick look in the mirror can be the most important thing you do. Take this quiz when deciding what to wear:

1. Did I remember to wear a comfortable dress, skirt, or shirt and pants (and tie if I'm a guy)?
2. Is my dress or skirt at or below the knee?
3. Did I remove any distracting jewelry?
4. Is the neckline so low that cleavage is showing?
5. Should I wear hose or tights?
6. Are my shoes comfortable but still considered dress shoes?
7. Is the skirt, shirt, or blouse too fitted?
8. Did I conceal my tattoos?
9. Is my hair, jewelry, and cologne conservative and not distracting?
10. Would I hire me based on my appearance today?

Professional dress is important to a future teacher because it helps you project a professional image. Do you want to be taken seriously by your students? Do you want to make a great impression? Professional appearance will play a huge role in your being hired. Asking yourself the previous questions before you go into a classroom will help you establish your professional image and message. You are evolving from student to teacher, establishing your professional brand so that you will be treated as a professional in the workplace.

To learn more about teacher dress code tips, follow this link. https://www.youtube.com/watch?v=XKh1YQly-nk

What about attire for those who teach physical education or whose cultural background or religious beliefs dictate a particular kind of dress? Obviously, exceptions and accommodations can be made. Become aware of expectations in districts where you want to live and work. Talk with school administrators. Know what to expect and learn how you will be perceived before you show up at a school.

Question # 16

Is Teaching a Job or a Profession?

Teaching creates all other professions.

—Unknown

What spurred your interest in teaching? Have you always loved learning, and do you want to instill this passion in others? Is there a great teacher in your past who served as a powerful role model you want to emulate? Have you thought about whether you view teaching as a job or as a profession? Do you think there is a difference?

A profession is often described as a broad field that requires formal qualifications and training, while a job is described more narrowly, as a position in which you are paid for a service, often at an hourly rate. You could also think of a job as short-term, while a profession is a lifelong commitment and career. You start on a career path by learning about yourself, identifying your skills, learning about your values, researching career options, and linking a major to a career. High school and college students are at the beginning of this process. As you hone your skills in education classes, and later in your own classroom, learning and teaching will become more intertwined. You will begin to learn the art of teaching as you study educational research and methodologies. As you are placed in classrooms and work with mentor teachers and students, you will become part of the learning/teaching cycle, where you are both the learner and the teacher. You will then become a professional, a practitioner who loves learning and enjoys sharing that experience with others. Teaching is not a job where you learn a set of skills and repeat them throughout the day. To be a successful teacher, you must think of yourself as a problem-solver who is motivated to keep learning.

Do you have the growth mindset to be a life-long learner? How comfortable are you with the idea that teaching is a profession and not just a job? Young educators leave the profession at an alarming rate, with numbers ranging from 17 to over 40 percent within the first five years of joining the profession.[10] New teacher departures, especially in urban

---

10   http://www.gse.upenn.edu/pdf/rmi/PDK-RMI-2012.pdf

and rural areas, are outpacing retirements of veteran teachers. Many new teachers say they leave because they found teaching to be an isolating, stressful "sink or swim" experience. Other reasons teachers give for leaving the profession include unrealistic federal and state mandates, lack of support, student discipline challenges, low pay, and lack of influence and respect.

Given these challenges, what makes you think you have what it takes to stay in the profession for more than five years? In the style of blue-collar comedian Jeff Foxworthy, reflect on these ideas:

- If you want a profession where you get paid for eight hours a day, five days a week and then work for free at night, on the weekends, and in the summer rather than work a job for eight hours, five days a week with the summer off…then you might be a teacher.
- If you want a profession where you are so interested in learning that you will take your vacation time to attend classes at your own expense rather than actually go somewhere on a trip…then you might be a teacher.
- If you are okay with the idea that you will be compensated for your professional knowledge at a set salary regardless of the time you spend rather than work a job where you are compensated by the hour for the work you actually do…then you might be a teacher.
- If you like to identify problems and search for solutions rather than let others solve your problems for you …then you might be a teacher.
- If you are comfortable taking risks and accepting responsibility rather than sitting back and letting others be responsible for outcomes…then you might be a teacher.
- If you are willing to stay longer, work harder, and get smarter rather than just get by doing the bare minimum requirements … then you might be a teacher. And, you might make it beyond five years.

If these descriptions of the teaching profession don't make you balk, then you will likely be a good teacher.

To learn more about trends in the teaching profession, follow the links to these websites.
https://twitter.com/search?q=teaching+profession&ref_src=twsrc%5E google%7Ctwcamp%5Eserp%7Ctwgr%5Esearch
https://www.youtube.com/watch?v=m6nyz1JdzXQ

Reference
Ingersoll, R. (2012). Beginning teacher induction: What the data tell us. Phi Delta Kappan, Vol. 93, No. 8, p. 47-51.

Question # 17

Do Teachers Always Have to Tell the Truth?

No legacy is so rich as honesty.

—William Shakespeare

Watch your thoughts; they become words. Watch your words; they become actions. Watch your actions; they become habits. Watch your habits; they become character. Watch your character; it becomes your destiny.

—Frank Outlaw
Late President of the Bi-Lo Stores

As a future teacher, you want to gain the trust of those around you. One way you build this trust is by being honest. You have probably heard the expression, "Honesty is the best policy." Do you hold yourself to this standard, or are you only honest when it is convenient, either personally or professionally, for you to do so? Do your friends ask for your opinion? When asking for their opinion, are you interested in hearing what your peers really think, or do you just want them to tell you what you want to hear? Have you ever asked a professor to give you feedback when it was not required? Is there ever a time not to say what you really think? The pursuit of honesty sounds complicated. So, where should you begin?

Academic institutions have academic honesty/dishonesty policies. Are you familiar with those policies? If not, familiarize yourself with your student handbook. A course syllabus also includes important statements regarding academic dishonesty. Common examples of dishonesty include cheating and plagiarism. Examples of cheating could include copying exams, papers, or assignments; allowing another student to copy your work; or taking a test for another student. Plagiarism could include submitting a paper written by another student or failing to cite sources in a paper. But there are others ways to be dishonest. Faking the results of an experiment, writing in an observation journal or reflection about events that never happened or you never observed, or saying you taught a lesson and never did are all dishonest behaviors. Giving a false excuse for missing a test, pretending to have previously submitted assignments, pretending to be sick or giving some other excuse for not attending class, creating a lesson plan after you have taught a lesson rather than using it as the way it was intended, which is as a preplanning tool, are also examples of deception and dishonesty.

So, what can you do now to help you prepare for the future? Follow these strategies to put your honesty into action.

- Develop a reputation for being honest by adhering to your academic institution's policies regarding academic honesty.
- Prepare for assignments so that you are not tempted to cheat or lie.
- Don't enable other students to be dishonest by lending them your papers or assignments or allowing them to copy from your exams.
- Report incidents of academic dishonesty to your instructors.

Honesty also includes being yourself. Your words, actions, and appearance should reflect accurately who you are. Be honest about your feelings with your mentors and instructors. Address issues when you feel intimidated or have a fear of saying or doing something stupid. When speaking, stay true to the facts. Be open, sincere, and direct in your discussions with others. During class discussions, listen to what others have to say. Speak honestly and accept feedback. Build trust so you don't offend or embarrass others as you speak. Don't forget to seek feedback from your mentor about your abilities.

In the teaching profession, employers are looking for someone who has a reputation for being honest. Good student-teacher relationships come from mutual respect and trust.

To learn more about the value of honesty, follow the links to this website.
http://www.values.com/inspirational-stories-tv-spots/91-classroom

Question # 18

Are You Coachable?

The mind is like a parachute. It only works when it's open.

—Unknown

Do you have experience in team sports, music, or drama? Would others describe you as a team player? Do you seek help so you can improve your skills? Or, would others describe you as a loner? Do the words, "I guess you will just have to learn it the hard way" sound familiar?

Coaching is support and guidance given to others. It is using existing knowledge and skill more effectively to improve performance. It consists of coach-to-student as well as peer-to-peer discussions. Coaching provides descriptive, direct and honest feedback about an individual's strengths and weaknesses.

Employers are interested in your interpersonal skills as well as your intellectual skills. Does your resume contain adequate examples of your active engagement in sports, music, drama, clubs, or special interest activities? Your involvement in extracurricular activities will be reviewed to determine how you respond to coaching. Do you listen, respond to constructive criticism, show a growth mindset, and stick with challenges? In her book *Grit: The Power of Passion and Perseverance*, Angela Duckworth provides a Grit Grid that aspiring teachers should utilize to maintain a record of their accomplishments in high school and, especially, college (see Table 4.1).

You are coachable if you are asking questions and seeking guidance so that you can reflect on the knowledge, skills, and dispositions you need to become an effective teacher. You are coachable if you accept advice from others, practice, and then set goals to improve. You are coachable if you seek out experts and initiate discussions by asking questions and listening to their answers. You are coachable if you take ownership of what is defined as your strengths and needs and establish goals for improvement.

Traits exhibited by coachable teacher candidates include
* humility - demonstrated through willingness to change your behavior and outlook.
* flexibility - shown when working with others to accomplish mutual goals.

- selflessness - displayed by being willing to relinquish control and working within a group.
- confidence - gained by trusting in the abilities of a group or team.
- persistence and grit – revealed over time through a desire to achieve your best.

Additionally, you can prepare to be a coachable teacher by focusing on the following:
- Make a list of your strengths and needs.
- Set a goal.
- Look for feedback from peers and knowledgeable others.
- Ask someone to coach you.
- Ask questions.
- Don't interrupt.
- Listen. Listen. Listen.
- Accept constructive feedback and use it to improve.
- Commit the time to improve knowledge and skills.
- Seek out experiences in group activities in sports, music, and the arts.

Finally, understand what it means to possess the characteristics of a growth mindset and to master the power of deliberate practice by overcoming the toughest challenges you face, embracing the advice of others, and learning from their experiences. Then, you will be well on your way to being the best you can be.

TABLE 4.1

THE GRIT GRID

List activities (sports, music, drama, volunteering, hobbies, paid work) in which you devoted a significant amount of time outside class.

Activity	Grade You Participated				Achievements, Awards, Leadership Positions
	9	10	11	12	
1.					
2.					
3.					
4.					

Adapted from *Grit: The Power of Passion and Perseverance* by Angela Duckworth, (2016). p. 231.

Kids who spend more than a year in extracurriculars are significantly more likely to graduate from college and, as young adults, to volunteer in their community. The hours each week that kids devote to extracurriculars also predict having a job (as opposed to being unemployed as a young adult) and earning more money, but only for kids who participate in activities for two years rather than one.

Reference

Margo Gardner, Jodie Roth, and Jeanne Brooks-Gunn. "Adolescents Participation in Organized Activities and Developmental Success 2 and 8 Years After High School: Do Sponsorship, Duration, and Intensity Matter? *Developmental Psychology* 44 (2008): 814-30.

CHAPTER 4

DISCUSSION QUESTIONS & PERSONAL IMPROVEMENT ACTIVITIES

1. Conduct your own personal background check via Google and social media. What do you discover about your web footprints? Is it professional? Does anything need to be deleted?

2. Make a list of the people you would ask to write a letter of recommendation or act as a reference. Do not include family members or close personal friends. Who can play the most influential role in helping you get the job of your dreams?

3. Describe a time you were at a social event and wish you weren't. What happened as a result?

4. Discuss some of the personal choices you have made recently. Will they help or hurt you as you enter the teaching profession?

5. Check out a future employer's webpage and see if there is a dress code or code of conduct. Do you find any red flags?

6. If you have tattoos or piercings, how are you going to explain them to potential employers who might view them negatively?

7. Would you describe yourself as a life-long learner? If so, what examples could you give?

    a)

    b)

    c)

8. Do you know the average minimum salary of a teacher in your local area?

9. What would you wear to an interview or the first week/month of school?

10. Has there ever been a time when you wished you had spoken-up to defend your point of view or that of a friend or colleague? Has there ever been a time when you wished you had listened better? Give examples.

a)

b)

c)

11. Give an example of how and when someone coached you through a self-improvement process.

CHAPTER 4 SELF-ASSESSMENT

HOW TO USE THIS ASSESSMENT GUIDE

Aspiring teachers are nurtured and supported through strong relationships. You should reflect privately, but you should also seek the perspective of and advice from teachers, professors, counselors, parents, friends, and others who can help you discern your personal and professional capacities as you prepare to become a teacher. There are no right answers. Be honest with yourself. When you are finished with this chapter, discuss your self-evaluation (see the chart below) with the people supporting you. Together, your self-evaluation and subsequent discussions should reveal strengths as well as areas for further growth.

If you frequently engage in reflective activities, you should be well prepared for any outcomes of formal evaluation practices.

My preparation and/or professional performance skills indicate that ...	Strongly disagree	Disagree	Neutral	Agree	Strongly agree	No Opinion/ No Response
13. I have no problems passing a background check.						
14. My tattoos and piercings, if any, are appropriate for the teaching profession.						
15. I understand and respect professional attire and decorum for a career in teaching.						
16. I believe that teaching is a profession.						

17. Teachers must always be honest.						
18. I have experience in activities where I have proven to be coachable.						

CHAPTER 5

INITIATIVE

In the Oxford Dictionary Online, definitions of the word *initiative* include

- the power or opportunity to act or take charge before others do.
- an act or strategy intended to resolve a difficulty or improve a situation; a fresh approach to something.
- the ability to assess and initiate things independently.

Aspiring teachers should review the following questions, which are based on the ones Eric Chester asks in his book *Reviving Work Ethic: A Leader's Guide to Ending Entitlement and Restoring Pride in the Emerging Workforce* (p. 135). [11]

1. What does initiative mean to you?
2. What does initiative mean in the college classroom? Cite three examples.
3. What role does initiative play in creating passion for teaching?
4. How does initiative interplay between fixed and growth mindset?
5. What motivates you to become a teacher?
6. What are some benefits of showing initiative in a clinical teaching setting?
7. How curious are you about emerging education theories?
8. What aspect of teaching do you like most?
9. Can you cite concrete examples of how you have taken the initiative in your preparation to become a teacher?
10. What prevents you from showing initiative?

The questions in this chapter are intended to help you think about, understand, and develop observable behaviors and actions related to the concept of initiative that every effective teacher must possess. Find multiple ways to reflect, discuss, and plan to assure that you develop high levels of ambition, curiosity, and initiative in your own unique way.

---

11   http://www.oxforddictionaries.com/definition/english/initiative

Question # 19

Are You Motivated?

We are what we repeatedly do. Excellence, then, is not an act, but a habit." –
—Aristotle

Do you want to know who you are? Don't ask. Act! Action will delineate and define you.

`—Thomas Jefferson

Would others describe you as motivated? Are you productive, or do you procrastinate? Do people have to ask you multiple times to do something? Do you set goals and achieve them?

Motivation is a desire to act. People who are motivated set goals. Being highly motivated increases the amount of time and effort you are willing to spend on a project. Have you ever noticed how when you really want something you will work longer and harder to get it? Or, when you see the relevance in what someone is asking you to do, you are more engaged and successful?

Teachers are always looking for ways to increase motivation because there is a positive correlation between motivation and learning. Basic facts that aspiring teachers should know about motivation include the following:

1. There are two kinds of motivation: extrinsic and intrinsic.
   a. Extrinsic motivation comes from tangible rewards for a desired positive behavior (e.g., money or grades) or from the possible threat of punishment following misbehavior.
   b. Intrinsic motivation comes from intangible rewards, such as being driven by a desire to do well or by enjoyment of a task.
2. Social psychological research has shown that extrinsic rewards can lead to over-reliance, reducing intrinsic motivation.
3. The self-control aspect of motivation is increasingly considered to be a subset of emotional intelligence. Emotional intelligence (EI) is the ability to recognize your emotions and the emotions of others. If you have EI, then you have the ability to lead and motivate others.

4. Teachers should understand how to best utilize incentive theory promoted by behavioral psychologists such as B.F. Skinner, content theory of human motivation, such as Abraham Maslow's hierarchy of needs, and Herzberg's two-factor theory. Maslow's theory is one of the most widely discussed theories of motivation. (See Figures 1 and 2).
5. Sufficient sleep enables individuals to stay highly motivated.
6. Motivating ourselves with external rewards (the carrot and stick approach) is difficult to sustain.

Understanding motivation helps explain behavior. It tells use why we act the way we do, and why we have desires and needs. Motivation is one of the most studied and popular psychological concepts. To get you thinking about your life, your goals, your habits, and how you might increase your motivation to become a teacher, consider this advice:
- Focus on enjoying what you are doing right now.
- Think of every failure you experience as a learning opportunity.
- Set a goal and work hard to accomplish it. Success will motivate you to replicate the effort put forth to achieve the goal. Your confidence will grow.
- Find what works best for you and keep doing it.
- Keep yourself from feeling overwhelmed by focusing on doing one thing at a time. Focus on the positive.
- If you find yourself worrying, then focus more on what you're doing and less on what others are doing.
- Don't try to control others. You can't.
- Figure out what is distracting you and minimize it.
- Set aside time for important tasks. Don't try to multitask.

When you are passionate about your job, motivation is high. Develop your intrinsic motivation for teaching by cultivating a deep awareness and understanding of your purpose(s) as a teacher. For most, money is not a motivator. What drives you? Why do you really want to be a teacher?

To learn more about motivational theory, follow this link.
http://www.edpsycinteractive.org/topics/motivation/motivate.html

How motivated are you? Take the mindset quiz at
http://www.mindtools.com/pages/article/newLDR_57.htm

FIGURE 5.2

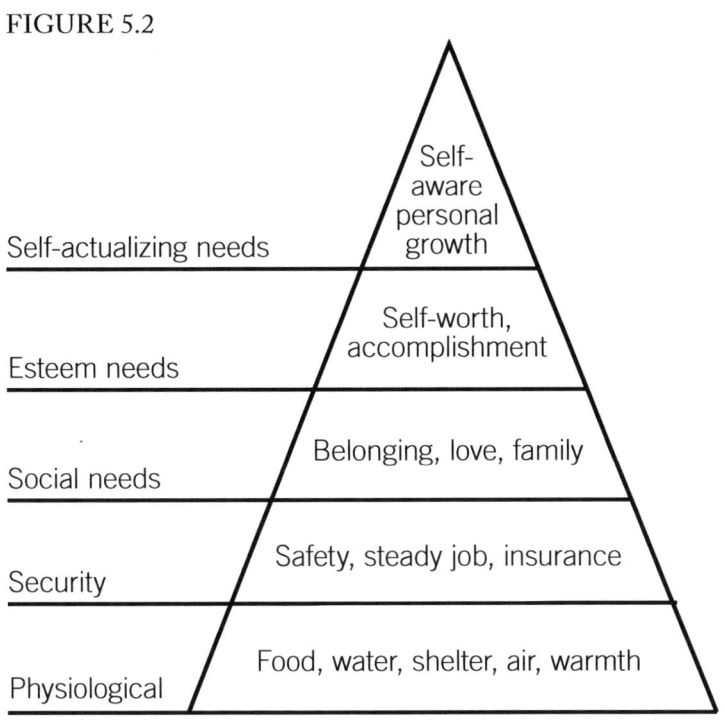

Maslow's hierarchy of needs (1943)

Question # 20

Do You Have Curiosity and Know How to Ask Questions?

Judge a man by his questions rather than by his answers.

—Voltaire

Do you have curiosity? Everyone knows the saying "curiosity killed the cat," but maybe a better saying would be "a lack of curiosity killed the cat," or at least, made it extremely bored.

Curiosity is a natural part of childhood. Children explore their surroundings and enthusiastically go outside and play. If you've been around young children, you know there is a constant litany of "why?" questions when they are trying to understand a concept.

So why do many adults lose their curiosity? Why do they forget to question what is in front of them? Not being curious leads to compliancy and resistance to change. Have you ever read something, and it just doesn't pass the smell test? You know some fact doesn't add up, but you accept it as true, despite an inner voice telling you not to, because everyone else has accepted it too.

How can you stay curious as a teacher? There are different types of questions that you should be asking yourself daily. They are the "why?" "how?" and "so what?" questions. The "why?" question starts at a basic level. It initiates follow up questions. The "how?" question builds another layer, exploring in the physical sense or searching for information in the cognitive sense. "So what?" questions take curiosity to the highest level. In the following table, sample questions about snakes in Hawaii provide examples that develop higher levels of curiosity.

Why? Questions (or First Glances)	How? Questions	So What? Questions
Why are there no snakes in Hawaii?	*How did it happen that snakes do not live in Hawaii?*	*Why should I care if there are no snakes on Hawaii? So what?*
First glance would tell you that there should be snakes in Hawaii, as the topography should support this reptile. There are fresh water, grasses and a food source.	Through deeper research, you discover that the islands were formed from volcanic eruptions and were not part of Pangea, so snakes did not travel to the islands from other parts of the world.	You might develop higher levels of curiosity to determine whether other species are not found on the islands or developed differently there. The Nene duck, for example, cannot fly and has adapted to living on the islands.

By asking questions and demonstrating how to look for answers, teachers model curiosity and help students gain deeper insights into the world around them. Learn to ask good questions and maintain curiosity about the world around you.

Think about this. All great inventions in the world were once ideas. Ideas come from being curious and the continuous desire to know more. Instead of thinking "curiosity killed the cat," consider that "curiosity does not kill the cat, but nourishes it instead."

Have you ever been curious about these topics?

Question	Answer
Why did people in the late 1400s think the world was flat? Why did Christopher Columbus think differently?	Many explorers became lost at sea. As a result, perception was that they fell off the earth. Columbus' voyages led to discoveries and new maps.
How did Isaac Newton come to understand the law of gravity?	Newton explained the law of gravity as he saw apples falling to the ground. That type of curiosity led to more scientific discoveries.
Why was George de Mestral curious about the spurs that stuck to his clothes? What did his curiosity produce?	He invented Velcro, but it did not become popular until NASA used it on space suits.
What caused the man who was perhaps the greatest musician of all time to go completely deaf?	DNA testing of follicles of Beethoven's hair has shown that lead poisoning was the likely cause.
What concerns you about becoming a teacher? What should you do to address those concerns?	Talk with your professor(s) and mentor(s). Share your concerns openly and be receptive to feedback.

When asked, students will often say they don't ask questions in classes, not because they lack curiosity, but because they don't know what to ask or don't want to appear foolish in front of their peers. Professors, however, may perceive a lack of questioning as a lack of curiosity. Don't be afraid to ask questions. It is important to have two-way exchanges of information. Follow this guide for strategies to shape questions:

Types of Questions
Why – Why should we do this? Is there a rationale or evidence?
What – What are the exact meanings? Key terms? What is needed to complete work?
How – How do we proceed? Is there a preferred process?
When – When is this due? When do we find time?
Guiding – What is the key purpose? Key learning objectives? What are we to accomplish?
Quality – How is this being graded? How can we self-assess? Criteria?
Assurance – Suggestions for success? Cautions? Obstacles? Alternatives?

During or after interviews, many principals or interview teams ask candidates if they have any questions for them. For some, it can be a deal breaker if the candidate isn't prepared to ask any. Use these 10 questions as starters and develop your own list of potential questions.

1. What can I clarify that would make hiring me an easy decision?
2. What do you envision as most important to accomplish in this position right away?
3. What new teaching skills and strategies can I hope to learn here?
4. What is the biggest challenge facing this school? School district?
5. What is the best part of working here?
6. What is the worst part of working here?
7. Who is your ideal candidate, and how can I make myself like that ideal?
8. How did you get started in teaching?
9. What concerns/reservations do you have about me for this position?
10. How will my work contribute to the school's mission and vision?

Question # 21

Do You Have a Plan to Achieve Goals?

People with goals succeed because they know where they're going.
—Earl Nightingale, 1921–1989
American Radio Personality

How many times have you made a New Year's Resolution and then promptly forgotten about it? Have you ever written a goal down on paper, mapped out a series of steps to accomplish it, and then actually realized your goal? Do you have a plan in place to achieve goals in your personal and professional life?

Goals are outcomes you wish to achieve. Goal-setting is a powerful process that helps you turn dreams into reality. By knowing what you want to achieve, you know where you have to concentrate your efforts. Follow the acronym LEAD to set goals for your education, career path, financial security, family responsibilities, personal health, entertainment, and community service: [12]

Learn—determine strengths and weaknesses by analyzing, assessing, planning, and then implementing an action plan.

Evidence—demonstrate what you learn.

Attitude—make choices that demonstrate a positive work ethic and good character.

Decisions —show evidence of good decision making leading to the goal.

Brainstorm goals with friends and colleagues. Make goals more powerful by using the LEAD process and the SMART mnemonic.

S – Specific (or Significant)
M – Measurable (or Meaningful)
A – Attainable (or Action-Oriented)
R – Relevant (or Rewarding)
T – Time-bound (or Trackable)

---

12   Reeves, D. & Allison, E. (2009). *Renewal Coaching: Sustainable Change for Individuals and Organizations.* San Francisco: Jossey-Bass.

Goal setting is a powerful process that helps you separate what's important from what's irrelevant. It helps you stay on track so you don't get distracted. By knowing what you want to achieve, you can concentrate on these three questions: Where am I now? Where do I need to be? How will I get there? Goal setting has many benefits, including increasing your motivation, your efficiency, your self-confidence, and your self-esteem.

Here are some tips to help you achieve your goals:
- Keep your goals positive.
- Be specific so you can measure achievement.
- Set priorities so you stay focused on the immediate goal and don't get overwhelmed.
- Keep to-do lists so you have the steps written down to keep you focused.

If you don't already set goals, start today. Pick something you want to achieve and develop a plan to achieve it. Your success will feel great!

The South Central Kansas Educational Service Center provides an excellent template to assist with the writing of SMART goals:
www.sckesc.org/common/pages/DisplayFile.aspx?itemId=5137890

To learn more about goal setting, follow the links to these websites.
https://www.youtube.com/watch?v=8cCiqbSJ9fg
https://www.youtube.com/watch?v=1-SvuFIQjK8
https://www.youtube.com/watch?v=MZXHILQGquQ

Question # 22

Do You Know How to Click with People?

Anyone who has ever experienced love at first sight will tell you that the connection with the other person was instantaneous and magical. Something clicked. People who play on teams at high levels often attribute their success to the fact that the individual team members "just clicked." When teachers develop skills that enable them to click with students and parents in a quick and easy manner, they become expert at developing relationships. [13]

According to Ori and Ram Brafman, brothers and co-authors of *Click, the Magic of Instant Connections*, a click occurs between two people when their brains are fully engaged and resonating. Clicks shape our thinking, behavior, and emotions. They can be developed by focusing on five "accelerators" formulated and explained by the Brafmans:

1. Similarities—You might click with people with your same name, birthdate, home state, or other characteristic. Deciding to intentionally search for similarities prepares you for the second accelerator, resonance.
2. Resonance—This is where the magic happens, where you are fully present, in the zone, paying close attention to attitudes, emotions, and needs of others.
3. Proximity—You'll likely hit it off with people who are closest to you. If you always sit in the back row of a classroom, you stand to have fewer opportunities to click with your teacher. The adage "out of sight, out of mind" illustrates the need for proximity.
4. Vulnerability—When we choose to take the risk and open up to others about our insecurities, fears, and needs, we become more likely to connect with those who share similar concerns. By paying close attention to the way we communicate, we increase our abilities to connect on an emotional level.

---

13   The need for aspiring teachers to be able to build relationships is a theme interwoven in many of the questions in this book.

5. Situations—Often, unique circumstances we encounter can help nurture clicks. When we work together with others to overcome adversity and achieve goals, we can click as part of a team, a defined, shared community.

Some people appear to click with others easily. They know how to work a crowd. They monitor others closely and adapt their own emotions and communication style to align with those they are speaking to. Knowing how to ask questions in the right way becomes a powerful clicking initiative. Ask open-ended questions (ones that require more than a "yes" or "no" answer) that show you've been paying attention to the person or people you're talking to. Ask follow-up questions to show you've been listening carefully and want to know more.

When a teacher knows how to accelerate a click, they bring out the best in other people. Developing relationships does not have to be left to chance. Learning how to accelerate the development of personal connections can change the nature of the relationship, not only in the moment but for a lifetime.

The Brafmans illustrate the power of proximity by analyzing the strength and durability of the on-court connections and interpersonal communication skills exhibited by the Florida Gators basketball team during the 2006 and 2007 NCAA tournament seasons. The fact that four of the star players lived together in the same dorm, shared the same bathroom, and spent hours together even when they were not involved in a team practice helped them develop their "click," become close friends, and communicate effectively on and off the court. Many other coaches subsequently took note of a winning strategy discovered, not intentionally by coach Billy Donovan, but rather perhaps accidentally by a decision made by the University of Florida Student Housing Authority. (See Chapter 3)

Recommended Reading:
Brafman, Ori, and Brafman, Rom. (2010). *Click: The Magic of Instant Connections.* New York: Broadway Books.

Kirschner, Rick. (2011). *How to Click with People: The Secret to Better Relationships in Business and in Life.* New York: Hyperion.

CHAPTER 5

DISCUSSION QUESTIONS AND SELF-IMPROVEMENT ACTIVITIES

1. What is motivating you to become a teacher? Make a list of what attracts you to the profession.

   a)

   b)

   c)

2. Revisit your timeline for competing your degree, licensing, and getting a job. Are you still on track? Do you have a list of school districts that you are considering working in? Have you spent time visiting those districts and schools to get to know the staff?

Career Timeline			
Year	Essential Coursework	Degree Requirements/ Internships/ Licensure	Schools to Consider for Application
2_ _ _			
2_ _ _			
2_ _ _			
2_ _ _			
2_ _ _			

3. Practice "clicking" skills in classes outside those in your education major. Can you successfully strike up a conversation with a stranger using the suggestions outlined in Question # 22.

CHAPTER 5 SELF-ASSESSMENT

HOW TO USE THIS ASSESSMENT GUIDE

Aspiring teachers are nurtured and supported through strong relationships. You should reflect privately, but you should also seek the perspective of and advice from teachers, professors, counselors, parents, friends, and others who can help you discern your personal and professional capacities as you prepare to become a teacher. There are no right answers. Be honest with yourself. When you are finished with this chapter, discuss your self-evaluation (see the chart below) with the people supporting you. Together, your self-evaluation and subsequent discussions should reveal strengths as well as areas for further growth.

If you frequently engage in reflective activities, you should be well prepared for any outcomes of formal evaluation practices.

My preparation and/or professional performance skills indicate that ...	Strongly disagree	Disagree	Neutral	Agree	Strongly agree	No Opinion/ No Response
19. I am strongly motivated to become an excellent teacher.						
20. I am curious to learn new things, and I ask questions regularly in classes.						
21. I have a timeline for completing my teaching degree, licensure, and getting a job.						

22. I understand the concept of clicking and can effectively use the accelerators to build relationships.						

CHAPTER 6

READING/WRITING

Almost daily, teachers write notes, memos, emails, and reports, all of which require good writing skills. The quality of your writing will likely influence your selection for job interviews. Good skills are crucial to making a good first impression. Poor writing skills are often interpreted as signs of incompetence or lower intelligence.

Reading is an essential skill for every teacher. If you want to teach but do not like to read or write because you struggle with these skills, you should get extra support to develop them. Without good reading and writing skills, you will not be an effective teacher.

The questions in this chapter are intended to help you think about, understand, and become motivated to develop high-quality reading and writing skills. Please take time to review the reading recommendations in this book. Reading good books will expand your thinking and performance as a teacher.

Find multiple ways to reflect, discuss, and plan to assure that your reading and writing skills are top-notch.

Question # 23

What Do You Read?

Kids learn how to read by practicing. Deliberate, intentional reading practice is important at all grade levels. To effectively teach reading, teachers should themselves be passionate readers.

We recommend aspiring teachers read a wide variety of genres in order to gain knowledge not only in their chosen content area but others as well. Well-read teachers can converse with students and adults about a variety of topics.

Read the newspaper each day. Avoid allowing social media to be your only news source. Delve deeper into what you read by seeking out differing opinions and perspectives.

Teachers must model intentional, in-depth reading habits for their students. When students watch you read, it will inspire them to do the same. You should establish a daily reading schedule for both your personal and professional interests.

Reading must be a priority in your classroom and your school's culture.

> If reading is something you don't do or don't like to do, you must either work to improve or seriously consider another choice of profession.

Aspiring teachers should routinely request reading recommendations from their teachers, counselors, and other people of influence. You should become familiar with prominent professional associations and regularly peruse their websites for publications, blogs, resources, and information that can enhance your knowledge. Become familiar with educational jargon, acronyms, and lingo to increase your vocabulary.

Obviously, students have many reading assignments to complete for their schoolwork. To become an effective teacher, you must read more than your students' assignments.

In job interviews, expect to be asked what you are currently reading, as well as what you have read related to the field of education and for personal interest. A wise job candidate might determine if a school has a book study or reading club and read books school staff has been reading. This will help him or her make a connection with the staff during the interview process.

We hope we have convinced you of the need to develop a personal daily reading habit and continuously improve your reading skills. Good readers make great teachers!

Question # 24

Do You Write?

Like reading, writing enhances many skills required of teachers, such as communication, analysis, and critical thinking. Yet, at the college level, we see countless students who don't like to write because they think they aren't good at it, which is a common indication of a fixed mindset.

Remember that a fixed mindset can be changed. The development of writing skills requires practice. Those who read will discern patterns of writing that they like. We read to become writers and write to become better readers. There are many online resources to help writers. There are grammar websites, easy-to-use dictionaries, thesauruses, and more. Familiarize yourself with them and use them and other print resources for guidance when you write formally or informally.

The use of social media and texting has introduced many informal writing shortcuts, such as acronyms and lack of punctuation. Do not allow these to infiltrate your professional writing. Learn the difference between formal and informal writing and use words, style, tone, and punctuation that are appropriate for your audience and purpose.

Tip—It is never a good idea to send your college professors or school principal a message that starts with "Hey!"

Every principal's goal is to support teachers. However, it is extremely difficult to defend a teacher who sends parents handwritten messages explaining a homework assignment that are riddled with misspellings, incorrect grammar, or indecipherable cursive. The development of cursive writing is still an important skill for teachers.

Aspiring teachers should master keyboarding skills before college, even before high school. Know how many words you can accurately type per minute when you apply for teaching positions. You may be asked this information in a job interview.

While you are a student, take advantage of every opportunity to write. You must acquire extensive experience through your own initiative. Just as you must work to develop reading skills, set aside blocks of time each day for writing. Free yourself from distractions. Write a blog. Submit articles to professional journals. Write and publish books.

Writing must become a priority in your classroom and in your school culture.

Question # 25

How Extensive Is Your Vocabulary?

Can you define *pedagogy*? How about *curriculum*? Can you pronounce them correctly? As you prepare to become a teacher, these are two of the many hundreds of vocabulary words you must know and understand. You must also master the vocabulary for your chosen content area, including educational terms, teacher jargon, and acronyms

A good vocabulary helps you communicate effectively and provide clarity for students. It makes you a better reader and a better writer. It creates an impression of intelligence and increases your ability to grasp ideas and think logically, making you a more informed and involved teacher. A good vocabulary can also boost your powers of persuasion. Increasing vocabulary is a core part of every language arts class and an expectation of every college course. All teachers must have vocabulary acquisition skills and know how to teach them.

If you feel your vocabulary needs a boost, use the following tips:

1. Purchase a thesaurus and a dictionary (or utilize online versions of both).

2. Read books with a rich vocabulary. Look up words you don't know.

3. Sign up for free online vocabulary games and word of the day services (such as email services from websites like **Merriam-Webster.com**).

4. Pick up new words from teachers and the people you talk with and listen to.

5. Utilize new words in conversation with correct context 5–7 times to assure they become part of your memory.

There are many ways to determine the meanings of new words. You can use context clues, the words and phrases in sentences close to the new word, to guess a word's meaning. At least half of the words in the English language are derived from Greek and Latin. Being able to isolate the roots and understand their meaning can help you grasp the meaning of words before looking them up in the dictionary. And of course, using the dictionary is much easier if you also develop strong spelling skills.

Web Resource: 100 Words Every High School Graduate Should Know
http://www.houghtonmifflinbooks.com/booksellers/press_
    release/100words/

Teachers Must Be Proficient in Four Types of Vocabulary
- Reading vocabulary
- Listening vocabulary
- Speaking vocabulary
- Writing vocabulary

CHAPTER 6

DISCUSSION QUESTIONS AND SELF-IMPROVEMENT ACTIVITIES

1. Select a topic you know a lot about and video/audio record yourself for three minutes. Listen to yourself and note your strengths and needs, including eye contact.

2. Watch a television documentary about something that interests you and your friends. Keep a record of how many vocabulary words you each do not know. Follow up afterward and learn the meaning of the words.

3. Watch a television documentary about a topic that you and your friends know little about. Keep a record of how many vocabulary words you each do not know. Imagine how students in your classrooms might feel. Brainstorm ways that you can teach challenging words and topics to make the words relevant and meaningful. And of course, don't forget to follow up afterward and learn the meaning of the words.

4. For one week, keep a daily log of your reading. Then, extend that time.

5. Write a blog about your experiences as an aspiring teacher.

CHAPTER 6 SELF-ASSESSMENT

HOW TO USE THIS ASSESSMENT GUIDE

Aspiring teachers are nurtured and supported through strong relationships. You should reflect privately, but you should also seek the perspective of and advice from teachers, professors, counselors, parents, friends, and others who can help you discern your personal and professional capacities as you prepare to become a teacher. There are no right answers. Be honest with yourself. When you are finished with this chapter, discuss your self-evaluation (see the chart below) with the people supporting you. Together, your self-evaluation and subsequent discussions should reveal strengths as well as areas for further growth.

If you frequently engage in reflective activities, you should be well prepared for any outcomes of formal evaluation practices.

My preparation and/or professional performance skills indicate that ...	Strongly disagree	Disagree	Neutral	Agree	Strongly agree	No Opinion/ No Response
23. I read at least 30 minutes every day beyond required school reading.						
24. My writing skills are advanced for college-level work.						
25. I have an advanced mastery of basic vocabulary and my selected content area/ discipline.						

CHAPTER 7

PUBLIC SPEAKING

Public speaking skills are valuable in both your personal and professional life. Teaching requires daily public speaking (your classroom is a public area), so the development of high-level skills in this area will increase your confidence and reduce any anxiety you may have. Effective teachers conceptualize their mastery of public speaking as a set of essential skills that include

1. mindset.
2. preparation and practice (perseverance).
3. stage presence.
4. voice control.
5. eye contact.
6. body language.
7. energy and delivery.
8. relevance.
9. connecting with an audience (students).
10. teaching through powerful stories.

The questions in this chapter are intended to motivate you to improve the ways you speak. Teachers must be able to speak without grammatical errors, with correct pronunciation, and with confidence. You must develop your capacity to speak publically in a formal register to the same level as your reading and writing skills. Listening to and observing good and bad speakers will help you learn effective skills.

Find multiple ways to reflect, discuss, and plan to assure that you become comfortable speaking in your classes and in all public forums.

Question # 26

Can You Speak Without Using Like, Um, Yeah, So, You Know?

Take advantage of every opportunity to practice your communication skills so that when important occasions arise, you will have the gift, the style, the sharpness, the clarity, and the emotions to affect other people.

—Jim Rohn
American entrepreneur, author and motivational speaker

You probably spend a great deal of time communicating via text and tweet, but have you spent any time wondering if you can speak? Are you a good oral communicator? Do your presentations go well? How would you rate your speaking skills?

Public speaking has similarities with music, drama, or athletic performances. It requires skill. You can get better with practice. Deliberate practice is the key to improvement. Remember, if you adhere to a growth mindset philosophy, you can work to improve your skills and abilities in this area. Follow the tips that follow to get started:

- Master the basic rules of grammar and pronunciation. The online tools Grammar Girl (http://www.quickanddirtytips.com/grammar-girl) and Wikipedia (https://en.wikipedia.org/wiki/Main_Page) can help.
- Speak using complete sentences to help your listeners understand what you are saying.
- Eliminate fillers such as um and like by simply pausing. Slowing your rate of speech will give you time to think.
- Record your speaking voice while reading from a book or conversing with a group. Analyze and critique your speaking with an experienced teacher.
- Talk publically about your personal experiences and ideas. It is always easier to talk about what you know.
- Learn as much about any new subject matter as you can, because the more you know, the more comfortable you will be.
- Listen to what others are saying so when you speak, you will make sense and add to the conversation.

- Set a goal to speak in every class so that you get comfortable with everyone's eyes focused on you.
- Analyze the speaking skills of others by listening for rate, intonation, grammar, pronunciation, as well as style, tone, volume, and speed
- "Talk Like TED" by watching a video of a TED Talk.

Becoming an effective speaker takes time and practice. Just remember that every great speaker probably started out as a poor one. Think of teaching as a performance. Effective verbal communication will help you connect with your audience.

TED ED is a website that can help you develop your speaking skills and show you how you can learn to inspire others with your spoken words. http://larryferlazzo.edublogs.org/2009/06/03/the-best-teacher-resources-for-ted-talks/

You can obtain a free copy of *Speak More Effectively Part One— Public Speaking: A Quick and Easy Way!* an eBook available from Dale Carnegie at dalecarnegie.com
http://www.dalecarnegie.com/public-speaking-book-by-dale-carnegie/

Question # 27

Do You Have a Teacher Voice?

Remember the sound of a coach's voice? The cheerleader's voice? The nasal, monotone, boring teacher no one listened to?

You will use a teacher's voice when standing in front of your class. It's a professional voice, different in sound quality from your day-to-day speaking voice. Research shows the timbre of a teacher's voice has a dramatic impact on how children behave and learn. Three elements in direct, face-to-face communication impact your teacher voice: (1) words, (2) tone of voice, and (3) body language.

The best way to analyze your teaching voice is to record yourself regularly as you practice teaching. Work to develop vocal variety (tonal expressions) reflecting your passion. Practice timing. Know when to pause. Strategic silence can be more powerful than words. Practice to develop flexible speech rates. Seek medical advice for any identified vocal production issues.

Teachers need voice training. Learn breathing and postural habits that are essential for maintaining a pleasant teacher voice. Teachers need to be able to project their voice effectively in a variety of circumstances. When they do, students become energized, focused, and actively listen.

Effective teachers use a combination of body language, tone, and words. When they do, students become more engaged. If you think you lack a teacher voice, make a commitment to practice and adopt a growth mindset belief that you can improve. You will!

Here are some positive and negative vocal qualities.

Positive

- Volume level is effective.
- Dynamic contrasts accentuate meaning of words.
- Sound is natural, relaxed, and free.
- Words are pronounced correctly.
- Pacing shifts without effort.
- Voice makes an immediate good first impression.

Negative

- Too loud or too soft.
- Nasal qualities.
- Squeaky voice.
- Mumbling and monotonous.
- Hesitation; timidity.
- Inappropriate inflection at the end of sentences.
- Difficult to understand accent.
- Letter sound problems ('S' or 'R' or combinations).

Question # 28

Do You Suffer from Stage Fright?

The brave man is not he who does not feel afraid, but he who conquers that fear.

—Nelson Mandela

Everyone feels nervous from time to time while speaking in front of a crowd, but for some, it can be a terrifying or even debilitating experience. The clinical term for stage fright is performance anxiety. If you dread the thought of getting up in front of a group of people and performing, you are not alone. Millions of people suffer from performance anxiety. Athletes, musicians, actors, and yes, even teachers, can experience performance anxiety. In some cases, it can prevent you from doing what you enjoy and affect your decision to become a teacher. Worst of all, performance anxiety can negatively affect your self-esteem and self-confidence. Those with fixed mindsets tell themselves that they can never be comfortable speaking in public. Those with growth mindsets, practice, critique themselves, learn from mistakes, and steadily become comfortable speaking in any setting.

So, here's some bad news followed by some good news. The bad news is that teaching is a performance, and severe performance anxiety can mar the delivery of a lesson. The good news is that performance does improve with excitement (adrenaline flow). So, a little stage fright can be a good thing. There are skills you can learn to reduce and manage fear and anxiety when you are speaking in front of a group:

- Eliminate distracters, such as the tendency to rock, sway, wave your arms, move around pointlessly, or use verbal graffiti (filler words like uh and um that have no meaning).
- Continuously work to improve speaking or performance skills.
- Develop mindfulness, a state of active, open attention on the present ("with-it-ness").
- Shift the focus from yourself and your fear to your true purpose—teaching.
- Avoid thoughts about what might go wrong by focusing on concepts and images that are calming and reassuring.
- Refuse to think thoughts that create self-doubt and low confidence.

- Calm and relax your mind and body with deep breathing, relaxation exercises, yoga, and meditation.
- Exercise, eat well, and practice other healthful lifestyle habits. Limit caffeine, sugar, and alcohol as much as possible.
- Visualize your success. Always focus on your strengths and ability to handle challenging situations.
- Prepare your lesson in advance and rehearse it aloud to practice using effective vocal techniques.
- Make connections with your students. Smile.
- Stand or sit in a self-assured, confident posture. Remain warm and open, and make eye contact.
- Give up trying to be perfect, and know that it is okay to make mistakes. Individuals with growth mindsets learn from mistakes. Those with fixed mindsets avoid challenges, makes excuses, and never leave their comfort zone.
- Practice public speaking at every available opportunity.
- Seek feedback from a critical friend or mentor.

You have probably experienced some type of stage fright. It can be unnerving at times to be the center of attention, feeling that everyone is watching you. Your mouth goes dry and your knees, hands, and voice start to tremble. Most of these symptoms can be lessened with practice. Practice and adherence to a growth mindset philosophy *will* lead to improvement and success!

To learn more about speaking tips, follow the links to these websites.
https://www.youtube.com/watch?v=oGdO_3jlVas
https://www.youtube.com/watch?v=C1zY38pOLpw

According to Huffington Post, many celebrities, including stars such as Hayden Panettiere and Adele and more have suffered from stage fright but learned to deal with it.

(http://www.huffingtonpost.com/2013/04/05/celebrities-with-stage-fright_n_3022146.html?slideshow=true#gallery/290166/15

Question # 29

Can You Communicate with Your Eyes?

Almost nothing need be said when you have eyes.

–Tarjei Vesaas
Norwegian poet and novelist

Have you heard the expression, "The eyes are the window into the soul?" Nonverbal communication includes facial expressions. The eyes are powerful nonverbal communicators that can help or hurt the delivery of your message.

What kind of messages are you sending with your eyes? When you are speaking, do you have a hard time maintaining eye contact? When listening, do you spend more time looking at your hand-held electronic device than you do making effective eye contact?

By observing students' eye movements, teachers can see where students retrieve information. According to an approach to communication called neuro-linguistic programming (NLP), eye movements are linked to the following behaviors for right-handed people (they are reversed if you are left-handed):

- Up and to the right - remembering a picture image
- Up and to the left - constructing a visual image
- To the right - remembering sounds or conversations
- To the left - constructing sounds or conversations
- Down and to the right - experiencing an internal dialogue
- Down and to the left - accessing kinesthetic feelings, tastes and smells[14]

Establishing eye contact can help both the speaker and the listener. Eye contact can communicate respect, interest, appreciation, and understanding. When speaking to a group of people, imagine that you are having a conversation with one person at a time. As an example, focus on Person A as you finish an idea or make a point. As you begin a new idea or sentence, choose a Person B and establish eye contact. Continue this

---

14 http://files.eric.ed.gov/fulltext/ED508368.pdf

process until you have included everyone in the group, making sure not to single out any individual. If you are still having difficulty maintaining eye contact or finding a friendly face, try choosing a spot directly between or slightly above the listener's eyes to make your point. Maintaining good eye contact will make your listeners feel more comfortable. As your listeners feel more comfortable, your stress level will go down and you will feel more comfortable, too.

As a good listener, you should also show you are actively listening. Smiling, nodding your head, and maintaining eye contact will show that you are receptive to the speaker's message.

The following four strategies will help you work on good eye contact.
1. In every situation where you are the speaker, make eye contact with each person for 3–5 seconds.
2. Practice maintaining eye contact with yourself in a mirror, focusing for 3–5 seconds (so you have an idea of how long this is).
3. As a listener, look people in the eye when they are talking to you to avoid seeming aloof, uninterested, or confused.
4. Seek feedback from a friend or mentor after he or she has listened to your presentation or had a conversation with you.

Eye contact is a teacher's most important communication soft skill. Making eye contact when speaking must be a natural action. Eyes enhance conversations and make communication more effective. Students want and need eye contact from their teacher. Begin practicing now by maintaining appropriate eye contact with the people around you.

Web Resources

> To learn more about eye contact rules, follow the link to this website.
> https://www.youtube.com/watch?v=Ior3ilXjMTU

CHAPTER 7

DISCUSSION QUESTIONS AND ACTIVITIES

1. Closely observe several news anchors. What differences, good or bad, can you identify between how each one conveys messages with his or her eyes?

2. Watch any talk show. Do some of the show's hosts and/or guests present themselves as being more or less intelligent and prepared by their command of language and stage presence? What indicators do you observe?

    a)

    b)

    c)

3. Arrange to made a video recording of your next classroom presentation. Afterward, analyze it and count how many times you hear an ineffective use of *um, like, so, you know what I mean?* or any other form a verbal graffiti.

4. Watch public officials speaking to the media. Identify and analyze effective and ineffective practices.

5. Listen to interviews of coaches, athletes, and others who appear frequently to discuss their performances in unscripted settings. Analyze good and bad habits. Observe body language.

6. Practice staring at yourself in the mirror. Observe your eyes as you display the emotions listed in Question # 29. Pay close attention to your facial expressions and the muscles used. Your students will see and react to what you see. Practice so that eye contact becomes a strength.

CHAPTER 7 SELF-ASSESSMENT

HOW TO USE THIS ASSESSMENT GUIDE

Aspiring teachers are nurtured and supported through strong relationships. You should reflect privately, but you should also seek the perspective of and advice from teachers, professors, counselors, parents, friends, and others who can help you discern your personal and professional capacities as you prepare to become a teacher. There are no right answers. Be honest with yourself. When you are finished with this chapter, discuss your self-evaluation (see the chart below) with the people supporting you. Together, your self-evaluation and subsequent discussions should reveal strengths as well as areas for further growth.

If you frequently engage in reflective activities, you should be well prepared for any outcomes of formal evaluation practices.

My preparation and/or professional performance skills indicate that ...	Strongly disagree	Disagree	Neutral	Agree	Strongly agree	No Opinion/ No Response
26. I am an effective, confident speaker.						
27. In a professional setting, I can utilize a variety of vocal sounds and nuances resembling a teacher voice.						
28. I am confident, yet somewhat anxious, speaking in public forums.						
29. I maintain good eye contact and communicate visually in an effective manner.						

CHAPTER 8

PERSONAL CARE

Despite its many benefits, teaching can be stressful. To manage stress and take good care of themselves, effective teachers
1. adopt a growth mindset toward their work.
2. read and participate in other activities to expand their minds.
3. get plenty of sleep.
4. eat a balanced, nutritious diet.
5. exercise regularly.
6. connect with others in social settings.
7. effectively process emotions.
8. enjoy hobbies.
9. acknowledge the benefits of religion or spirituality.

Effective teachers prioritize self-care. The questions in this chapter are intended to help you learn the tools to maximize your own personal care. You must not be afraid to pamper yourself.

Find multiple ways to reflect, discuss, and develop personal habits that will ensure you have good health and the stamina to teach every day throughout your career.

Question # 30

Do Your Friends Bring You Down?

A real friend is one who walks in when the rest of the world walks out.
—Walter Winchell, Actor

Family members often ask each other "How was your day?" at the end of a work-day. Typical responses often reflect the day's social interactions. Interactions with your friends and peers can make you happy or drag you down.

If you watch the movie *Meet the Parents*, you'll observe Robert DeNiro's character talking about the "circle of trust." He is discussing the decisions people make about who they invite into their inner circle. The behavior of friends most often determines who stays or goes. According to Dr. Robin Dunbar, an evolutionary psychologist at the University of Oxford, adults need between three to five vital friendships for optimal well-being.[15] It only stands to reason that those friendships have strong enduring qualities, which are not possible to develop with mere acquaintances.

Everyone must ask important questions when considering whom to allow into an inner circle of friends. Perhaps most importantly, what do these individuals do for you? Do they help or hurt you? Are they trustworthy? Would you feel safe giving them access to your passwords or a key to your apartment? Is your association with them perceived well by your professors and other mentors?

Friendships change as people grow and mature. Friends who were important in high school may no longer share your life or career goals. It's important to reevaluate your friends as you make big life choices.

According to Suzanne Degges-White Ph.D., there are 13 essential friendship traits to consider when choosing friends for an inner circle.[16] How much importance do you place on each trait (described in Table 8.1)?

---

15   Rath, Tom. (2006) *Vital Friends: The People You Can't Afford to Live Without.* Gallup Press. http://www.psy.ox.ac.uk/team/robin-dunbar

16   https://www.psychologytoday.com/blog/lifetime-connections/201503/the-13-essential-traits-good-friends

TABLE 8.1

Friendship Trait	Unimportant	Little Importance	Neutral	Some Importance	Vital Importance
Trustworthiness					
Honesty					
Dependability					
Loyalty					
Trusting of Others					
Empathic					
Non-Judgmental					
Good Listener					
Supportive in Good Times					
Supportive in Bad Times					
Self-Confident					
Humorous					
Fun to Be Around					

As you reflect on your close friends, and even your family members, which traits are important to you? How would you rate your friends on meeting those qualities? If your close friends do not meet the standards that are most important to you, should they be in your inner circle?

Consider how these statements about friendships could affect your life.
- If your best friend eats a healthy diet, you are more likely to do the same.
- If you do not have a real friend at work, you have much less chance of feeling engaged.
- If you have a "best" friend at work, then you will more likely feel engaged in your job.

Since you are considering a profession in which you'll want to be productive and find self-fulfillment, you can see how important it is to develop and nourish friendships that support your aspirations.

Before takeoff, flight attendants inform passengers they should securely fit their own mask before helping children, the disabled, or persons requiring assistance. To many people, this suggestion seems somewhat counter-intuitive. However, trying to fit someone else's mask first puts you at risk for losing consciousness, making you incapable of providing help to anyone. Likewise, as a teacher, you can't care for your students if you don't care for yourself, first. And one of the most important self-care steps you can take is to surround yourself with friends who love and support you. Avoid people who drain your energy or confidence and put at risk your goal of becoming a great teacher.

Question # 31

Can You Manage Conflict?

Conflict only ever seems to resolve itself quick and predictably in thirty-minute sitcoms. In the real world, conflict can be messy and not easily solvable. All aspiring teachers should learn techniques for dealing with conflict.

Most people approach conflict according to their temperament, or biological disposition, which can be categorized into three types: (1) difficult, (2) slow-to-warm-up and (3) easy.

Teachers cannot choose to avoid dealing with conflict. It's inevitable, and it will occur with students, parents, and faculty. You can't easily change your feelings, but you can learn how to respond to conflict with adult behavior. This includes accepting the premise that conflict is a natural and inevitable occurrence that can sometimes end up being helpful. As a teacher, you must distinguish between conflict myths and realities (see Table 8.2).

Follow these tips to deal with conflict:
- Enroll in a conflict mediation program to learn necessary skills.
- Don't allow conflicts to fester.
- When facing conflict, make sure your communication is straightforward and concrete.
- Manage your emotions to resolve conflict successfully.
- Always strive to distinguish between the problem and the person. Focus on the problem, not the person. Try to look at the conflict from the other person's point of view.
- Understand the needs and interests that might lie behind concrete positions.
- Work to improve relationships.
- Realize that conflicts are an opportunity for growth. When you're able to resolve conflict in a relationship, it builds trust. You can feel secure knowing your relationship can survive challenges and disagreements

TABLE 8.2

Realities of Conflict	Myths of Conflict
Conflict is evitable.	Conflict will not happen if I prepare enough.
Conflict must be addressed in a timely fashion.	Conflict does not exist if I ignore it.
Conflict is a natural part of the classroom environment.	Conflict is not natural and can be overcome if the environment is managed sufficiently.
Conflict requires action on behalf of the students by the teacher.	I cannot change my biological temperament or my reactions to conflict.

Question # 32

Do You Have Work/Life Balance?

All work and no play makes Jack a dull boy.

—Proverb

Spending too much time working in your classroom without time away to rest and relax can make you both bored and boring.

Work life balance is perceived differently between people of different generations. Millennials, the youngest educators, currently work in schools with veteran teachers who are Baby Boomers or members of Generation X. The youngest generation (born from the late 90s until the present time, known as Generation Z or Homelanders), are just beginning to enter college and are in the process of experiencing the events that will help define them. Their perception of work and life is yet to be fully developed. (See Table 8.3 for general description of each generation.)

TABLE 8.3

Generation	Approximate Years	Work/Life Balance	Work Ethic	Perception of Work
Greatest Generation	1922–1945	Distinct separation between work and home life	Work hard; respect authority	An obligation
Baby Boomers	1946–1964	Balance tilted toward "Live to Work"	Workaholics; desire quality	An exciting adventure
Generation X	1965–1979	Balance tilted toward "Work to Live"	Skeptical; self-reliant in need of direction and structure	A difficult challenge; a contract
Generation Y Millennials	1979–1997	Balanced – other interests after work	Somewhat lacking; not content to "pay their dues"	A means to an end

Differing values and priorities among different generations in terms of work and personal fulfillment create the potential for ongoing conflict in schools. Baby Boomers sometimes perceive Millennials as less committed to their work. This perception may be based on evidence or on preconceived ideas. Millennials may have their own bias toward older generations. The truth is that there are hard workers and slackers among every generation in the workforce. What is important is that teachers, particularly aspiring teachers, set their own clear, realistic professional and personal goals. They need a focused career path (see Question # 21) consisting of incremental steps. In order to achieve balance, they must keep themselves physically and mentally fit. There needs to be a time to work and a time to play. Whatever your goals, you will need perseverance, grit, and a growth mindset to achieve them. Do not be too quick to judge older generations. Teachers who've been in the trenches for many years may make excellent mentors.

Remember the awesome seesaws on the elementary school playground? You may have had a wonderful experience when you and your friend were both pumping up and down in rhythm, steadied yourselves through balance, achieved maximum equilibrium in the air, and then communicated about how you were going to stop. However, if you really never had control and you couldn't trust your friend to stop gently, you most likely hit the ground with an hard thud! It takes practice to achieve balance.

Be wary of those who say they are burned out. It's highly improbable for a teacher to experience "burnout" if they've never "caught-on-fire" in the first place.

Question # 33

Are You a Multitasking Addict Tied to Your Cell Phone?

A person who is interrupted while performing a task takes 50% more time to complete it and makes 50% more errors.

— David Brooks
Writer, *New York Times*

We all multitask. Are these examples familiar to you?
- Studying while the television blares.
- Texting while driving.
- Operating a copy machine while eating lunch.
- Phoning while emailing or talking with friends.

You may be showing signs of abnormal cell phone usage if you exhibit some of the following symptoms:
- extreme anxiety when your phone is misplaced.
- uneasiness if more than two hours pass without checking your phone.
- anger when a cell phone connection is lost.
- compulsion to initiate and/or answer calls and text messages while driving.
- urge to check phone for messages upon waking.
- sleep next to a phone that is on and wake up to return late night texts.
- impulse to answer your cell phone while in an intimate embrace with a loved one.

A growing amount of research indicates that humans do not multitask as efficiently and effectively as we tend to believe. According to storyteller Amanda MacMillian, author Dave Crenshaw, neuroscientist Earl Miller, and even TV celebrity Oprah Winfrey, multitasking is a myth. MacMillian (2013) proposes twelve reasons not to multitask but rather to work on one task at a time.
1. You're really not multitasking.
2. It's slowing you down.

3. You're making mistakes.
4. It's stressing you out.
5. You're missing out on life.
6. Your memory will suffer.
7. It's hurting your relationships.
8. It can make you eat too much.
9. You're not actually good at it.
10. It's dampening your curiosity.
11. You can't OHIO—Only Handle It Once.
12. It can be dangerous.

Dave Crenshaw, in *The Myth of Multitasking: How "Doing It All" Gets Nothing Done*, explains how multitasking will wear you down, cause you to make mistakes, and result in less productivity. Particularly, Crenshaw expounds on passive and active switch-tasking, two concepts teachers deal with daily. Teachers must tell students when they can and cannot ask questions or interrupt. They must also tell students to complete one task before starting others. This lesson is one that all teachers struggle with and must constantly reinforce.

Despite what the research shows, teachers work in an environment where multitasking is essential. However, they must learn when to avoid it and rest. And they must teach students to limit time and use of technology when studying. Aspiring teachers should observe how master teachers deal with individual students with numerous needs—the active vs. passive switch-tasking concept.

If you recognize you have an unhealthy dependence on a cell phone, consciously modify your behavior toward more positive action. Train yourself to check for cell phone messages during appropriate times. Engage in face-to-face conversations more often than texting or interacting via social media. Show respect for others' time. Limit the hours that you use a cell phone. If you have an extreme case of unhealthy dependence, get professional treatment.

When you must, use your cell phone in private places (not in a public restroom, restaurant, class, church, or place where you must show respect for others). At work, show respect for your coworkers and boss, including everyone's need to get work done. Avoid unnecessary interruptions. Follow policies and guidelines for phone usage. Never look at a cell phone while teaching, attending a class or meeting, or driving. Cell phones are a great communication tool and a legitimate tool for learning. Just be sure to use them appropriately.

Recommended Reading
Crenshaw, Dave (2008). *The Myth of Multitasking: How "Doing It All" Gets Nothing Done*. San Francisco: Jossey-Bass.
MacMillian, Amanda. (2013). "12 Surprising Reasons Multitasking Doesn't Work" (www.health.com) "The Multitasking Myth" (Healthy Living)

Cautions for Teachers Using Cell Phones
1. If you wouldn't say it to your mother (or grandmother or others close to you), don't write it on Facebook, Twitter, or other forms of social media.
2. Everything school-related that you say or do on the web is archived (and can be subpoenaed in court). If you send a text or post to social media when you should be teaching, it can be traced.
3. Not sure you should text it? Don't!
4. Be careful not to be baited into responding to inappropriate social media posts by students and parents.
5. If digital bullies tell lies about you, seek counsel before taking any action.

Active versus Passive Task Switching

Following classes or professional presentations, people often seek out teacher(s) or presenter(s) with comments or questions hoping to learn more. While trying to respond, the teacher or presenter must simultaneously tear down equipment and pack up materials to get to their next class and to allow set up time for the next person using the space. In those situations, the teacher or presenter is likely forced to actively switch-task between multiple activities. As a result, the individual can be forced into a situation where he or she half-listens, provides inaccurate information, fails to effectively connect or click, and forgets to properly tear down and store away presentation equipment. Mistakes are often made while actively switch-tasking.

This happens to teachers when they allow students to interrupt while they are attempting to complete important tasks.

In contrast, people get more done with less stress and with greater accuracy when they learn how to passively and sequentially switch between important tasks.

When studying for a test, passive switch-tasking enables you to get more done, often in less time. Put away your phone, conveniently arrange all of your needed study materials, and work in a location without distractions. Social exchanges, interruptions, looking for materials, even glancing out the window eat up time and force you to reread and repeat work.

Question # 34

Do You Take Care of Yourself?

Teachers are role models for kids. You can't effectively teach kids the good habits and care for their bodies that they need to thrive if you don't first don't demonstrate that you can care for your own.

Aspiring and practicing teachers should:
* get 6–8 hours of sleep.
* eat a balanced diet.
* exercise regularly.
* maintain a healthy body weight.
* develop good habits (prudence, persistence, and organization).
* keep stress levels in check.

Teaching requires stamina. Teachers must always be at the top of their game. They need to continuously feed their minds, bodies, and souls.

Make a habit to maintain regular checkups with your doctor. Train your body's internal clock with regular sleep habits. Avoid fast foods and unhealthy eating habits/binges. Don't smoke or abuse illegal drugs. Limit intake of alcohol. Avoid unsafe sexual encounters. Deal effectively with stress, emotions, and mental health.

Accept the things you cannot change.

Test your cardiovascular strength and fitness with the STEP Test. All you need is a 12-inch high step and someone to time you.

Directions: Step on the block with your right foot and then with your left so that you are standing on the step, facing forward. Reverse, going down with your right foot and then the left. Repeat at a consistent pace for 3 minutes. Rest in a chair for one minute. Then take your pulse for six seconds and multiple that number by ten to determine your heart rate for one minute.

Results will vary depending on your age and gender. For men ages 18–25, a 60-second pulse rate between 85 and 100 is average to above average; 84 or less is good to excellent, while 101 or higher is fair to poor. For women ages 18–25, a 60-second pulse rate of between 94 and 110 is average to above average; 93 or lower is good to excellent, while 111 or higher is fair to poor. If you take the STEP test and you find yourself striving for more endurance, try the following:

I. Easy Level of Activity:
- Walking Briskly Outside
- Walking on a Treadmill
- Biking on Level Ground
- Treading Water in a Pool

II. Moderate Level of Activity:
- Biking on Paths
- Canoeing
- Dancing
- General Gardening
- Tennis (doubles)
- Water Aerobics

III. Advanced Level of Activity:
- Running
- Jumping Rope
- Martial Arts
- Race Walking
- Riding a Bike up Hills or Riding Faster
- Swimming
- Tennis (singles)

Source: Health.gov

Question # 35

Do You Have Test Anxiety?

The perfect is the enemy of the good.

—Voltaire

Making, taking, and giving tests are important teacher tasks. We live and work in an era where many tests are associated with high-stakes for students and teachers. For some, taking a test is as anxiety producing as speaking in public. It can also elicit other debilitating emotions, like increasing blood pressure, headache, nausea, shortness of breath, and more. Some might suggest that having a root canal is less stressful.

Many professional performers or athletes admit experiencing the "butterfly effect" before a major game or performance. They suggest that a little nervousness sharpens the mind and focuses attention. They develop routines that help them get in a performance state of mind, such as

- preparing efficiently over time.
- learning and doing relaxation techniques, such as meditation.
- getting plenty of sleep and exercise.
- eating and drinking appropriately.
- addressing any weaknesses or disabilities that can increase anxiety.

If necessary, they seek professional help to deal with high anxiety. But top performers cite deliberate practice, an intense focus on mastering the most challenging skills, techniques, or objectives, as their key strategy for alleviating anxiety.

After 2001, the No Child Left Behind Act (NCLB) raised state and federal testing requirements and accountability for the performance of all students. Standards and requirements for application in teacher preparatory programs also increased. In many cases, results from one high-stakes test heavily influenced promotion and retention decisions and limited who could and could not enroll in teacher education programs. The era of NCLB's influence is ending with calls for change driven by teachers who experienced students' meltdowns during high-stakes testing periods.

The Every Student Succeeds Act (ESSA, enacted in 2015) was designed to preserve annual assessments but reduce unnecessary and ineffective testing. Time will show us if the push back from NCLB requirements is enough to reduce concerns about what was declared to be widespread test anxiety.

Regardless of how ESSA is interpreted through state-by-state implementation, aspiring teachers must be able to pass required tests (ACT, SAT, Praxis, etc.) for admission into college programs. Likewise, they must know how to create formative and summative assessments (formative is ongoing, summative is the end product) in a variety of different formats and utilize test data to drive planning and instruction. They must understand and use Bloom's Taxonomy, Webb's Depth of Knowledge (DOK), etc. to gauge students' levels of understanding and comprehension in order to design effective formative assessments. Additionally, they should utilize formative instructional practices (FIP) that include learning targets and assessment processes to gather and respond to evidence about student learning.

Written assessments are only one method of determining student progress. Authentic performance should not be disregarded. Effective teachers instill their students with growth rather than fixed mindset skills. Those with growth mindsets learn how to respond to failure and realize that with hard work and persistence—the grit factor—achievement levels can be increased.

The future of aspiring teachers will still be influenced by tests. Using effective preparatory practices that can lessen anxiety, aspiring teachers should expect to be able to

- attain adequate scores on required assessments for teacher candidacy.
- distinguish what makes a good vs. bad test (content, set-up, aesthetics, ease of grading), which is a requisite part of every effective preparatory program.
- develop assessments in different forms (tech, authentic, etc., not just written).
- create and use a rubric.
- provide their students with various forms of feedback.
- address issues and determine personal ethical response to grading.
- proactively gain control of lingering, personal test anxieties.

CHAPTER 8

DISCUSSION QUESTIONS AND SELF-IMPROVEMENT ACTIVITIES

1. Pick a day and keep a total of how many minutes you are on your phone. What else could you do in the same amount of time?
2. Select ten adjectives you would use to describe a friend. If you find yourself struggling to come up with ten positive adjectives and instead find you are listing negatives, then maybe it's time to re-evaluate your friendship.
3. The first year of teaching has been described as a "sink or swim" experience. Make a list of friends you would want to include in your own "Survivor" episode.
4. Make a two-column chart (see example) with personal goals on one side and professional goals on the other side. Talk with a friend or colleague about where to start.

	Personal Goals	Due Date		Professional Goals	Due Date
1.			1.		
2.			2.		
3.			3.		
4.			4.		
5.			5.		

5. Join a Twitter chat at #ohedchat…
6. Check out the Ohio Student Education Association website at https://www.ohea.org/ (or search for your state's affiliate organization).
7. Join a professional organization such as the National Association for the Education of Young Children (NAEYC) or the Association for Middle Level Educators (AMLE) or a content-specific organization for higher grades.
8. Go to your state education website, locate the credential page, and take a practice test in your content area for your state licensure.

CHAPTER 8 SELF-ASSESSMENT

HOW TO USE THIS ASSESSMENT GUIDE

Aspiring teachers are nurtured and supported through strong relationships. You should reflect privately, but you should also seek the perspective of and advice from teachers, professors, counselors, parents, friends, and others who can help you discern your personal and professional capacities as you prepare to become a teacher. There are no right answers. Be honest with yourself. When you are finished with this chapter, discuss your self-evaluation (see the chart below) with the people supporting you. Together, your self-evaluation and subsequent discussions should reveal strengths as well as areas for further growth.

If you frequently engage in reflective activities, you should be well prepared for any outcomes of formal evaluation practices.

My preparation and/or professional performance skills indicate that ...	Strongly disagree	Disagree	Neutral	Agree	Strongly agree	No Opinion/ No Response
30. My friends are good influential, supportive, inspiring, and respectable role models.						
31. I am confident managing conflict. Conflict can be good.						
32. My personal and professional commitments are effectively balanced.						

33. I understand the dangers of a cell phone addiction and the inefficiency of multitasking. I know how to implement active vs. passive switch-tasking at appropriate times.						
34. I have routine physical exams, exercise regularly, eat a healthy diet, maintain good sleep patterns, and avoid bad habits.						
35. I understand strategies for test taking and do not suffer test anxiety.						

CHAPTER 9

PREPARATION

Avoid the temptation to place blame on your college or your former teachers if you find yourself unprepared for the demands of the career that lies ahead. You share much of the responsibility for your own learning.

To a large degree, your mindset philosophy will influence how well you plan, practice, and prepare to become a teacher. When college professors are asked to provide professional references for their students, the principals and personnel directors they speak with want to hear more about how you have comprehended, practiced, and developed the soft character skills you will need to succeed than the scores you have attained in math, or reading, or writing.

Principals and curriculum specialists will ensure you know the curriculum, pedagogies, and strategies they prefer. Without a doubt, you need to be competent in your content area. However, those skills alone will not be enough.

The questions in this chapter and throughout this book are intended to help you understand the importance of preparing your hard skills (those related to your cognitive abilities and content knowledge) and your soft character skills (those related to mindset and grit).

Find multiple ways to reflect, discuss, and plan strategies that will make you a well-prepared teacher.

Question # 36

Can You Envision Professional Career Steps?

Leadership is not about titles, positions or flowcharts. It is about one life influencing another.

—John C. Maxwell

Imagine that you have fast forwarded to the end of your college preparation, completed successful job interviews, and acquired your first teaching job. Congratulations! You've become a teacher! Your parents have bought you a fancy nameplate for your desk. A new school year, your first, is about to commence. Now, what?

You are expected to teach a class of young learners—and be their leader.

Many of John Maxwell's books are focused on leadership and have wonderful applicability for teachers. In *Leadership 101*, he states that no one is able to lead without first acquiring some form of influence. He affirms that everyone is, in some manner, a leader because everyone has influence over someone. Leading a classroom is all about gaining influence. Teachers must view themselves as influential leaders and learn how their level of influence can evolve as their professional career develops.

Try to envision your career path as a set of steps. On your first day of teaching, students eagerly file into your classroom. Your polished desk nameplate indicates that you are "teacher," but you must become more than that to be effective and to thrive. Even though you've worked hard for many years to earn your teaching credentials, students will quickly size you up (maybe within less than a minute) and decide if they think you'll make a good teacher. You are at the first step of acquiring influence.

Maxwell expertly explains how relationships are forged and outlines a total of five influential steps everyone must move up to effectively lead a business, a school, a classroom, or any enterprise. The steps, in order of progression, are:

1. **Position Level** (where you earn your degree, credentials, and license). Too many leaders (teachers) get stuck at this level because their students can detect a deficiency in their preparation or competence. If you are weak in content knowledge, use incorrect

grammar, show a lack of direction or self-control—any weaknesses in what are expected standards of preparation for a teaching position —you will likely move no further and not enjoy life as a teacher.

At the position level, <u>students attend your class because they have to.</u>

2. **<u>Permission Level</u>** (where your primary focus becomes building relationships with students, staff, parents, and community members, including gaining their permission to be a teacher). Assuming you can prove your competence for your position and pass everyone's first impression test, you should become focused on building relationships. In order for you to gain effectiveness as a teacher, your students must "let you in" and feel they can trust you. You must be a good communicator. Your position as a teacher requires spending varied amounts of time with different individuals (sometimes months or years), and you must realize that you can't move forward in a career without a sustainable record of building successful relationships. Every time a new student enters your class or a new school year begins, the process of moving up the steps of influence begins all over.

At the permission level, <u>students attend your class because they want to.</u>

3. **<u>Production Level</u>** (where, built upon a solid foundation of position and permission, you attain results). When you are widely recognized for competence and students welcome you into their lives, you'll get the results—student achievement—every teacher aspires to attain. Effective teachers should feel comfortable at this level after five years of teaching. Why do so many young teachers leave the profession at this point? It is because there are identifiable weaknesses at positions (steps) 1 or 2.

    If you gain a reputation of consistently getting outstanding results, expect to be sought out by others or moved to a location where your expertise is needed. In a new position, you must begin moving up the steps of influence all over.

At the enjoyable and fulfilling production level, <u>students attend your class because they want to because they see results.</u>

4. **People Development** (the focus changes to developing, or mentoring, students for the world of work, or college). Students who attain beneficial results under your tutelage may not want that relationship to end at the end of a school year. So, a teacher becomes a mentor and does what is necessary to nurture and guide students to achieve their dreams. Mentors and mentees willingly learn together, and their relationships become ever more meaningful. It takes years to acquire the reputation and credibility to become a competent, trusted mentor.
   When you gain influence and responsibility for developing others, students actively seek your guidance as they prepare to become future teachers or to pursue any other career.
5. **Personhood Level** (the pinnacle point of your career). After decades of influential, fulfilling work, those who reach the pinnacle of their career become sought-after consultants and recognized leaders within the profession. When they retire, buildings are renamed (or other celebratory actions taken) in their honor.
   When you've reached personhood, your former, now highly successful students, come back to find you wherever you go to seek your counsel and advice.

TABLE 9.1

Step 5 Personhood - *Students respect what you represent. You consult.*   (Respect) – *Teachers are at the pinnacle of their career.*
Step 4 People Development - *Students attend your class because of what you do for them.*   (Reproduction) – *New teacher mentoring occurs.*
Step 3 Production - *Students want to attend your class because they see benefits.*   (Results) - *If steps 1 or 2 are weak, you'll never get to this level.*
Step 2 Permission - *Students attend your class because they want to.*   (Relationships) - *The most challenging step for teachers who struggle with people skills.*
Step 1 Position - *Students attend your class because they have to.*   (Rights) - *Influence at this level is limited by a job description.*

So, what are the takeaways of Maxwell's steps of influence and career outline for an aspiring teacher? As Table 9.1 demonstrates, a teacher's level of influence affects his or her relationships with students, character development, and academic and behavioral outcomes. Before you begin a teacher preparation program, you must understand that your ability to get results will be severely limited by a lack of preparation to fulfill your job responsibilities and/or an inability to develop effective relationships. Too many teachers expect results from students without paying proper attention to the demands embedded in steps 1 and 2. The art of building relationships is the most challenging aspect of acquiring influence.

The questions and advice presented in this book will help you develop effective relationships and work your way up the steps of influence. After years of commitment and hard work, you'll reach the pinnacle step.

References and Recommended Reading:

Maxwell, John (2002). *Leadership 101: What Every Leader Needs to Know.* Nashville: Thomas Nelson Publishers.

Maxwell, John (2003). *Relationships 101: What Every Leader Needs to Know.* Nashville: Thomas Nelson Publishers.

Maxwell, John (2008). *Mentoring 101: What Every Leader Needs to Know.* Nashville: Thomas Nelson Publishers.

> Educators take something simple and make it complicated. Communicators take something complicated and make it simple.
>
> —John C. Maxwell

Compare achieving your career goals with how a baby first learns to climb up a set of stairs. What may appear to be daunting and dangerous becomes possible. The skillful ascension of that first step is an accomplishment parents proudly celebrate, and what the child instinctively learns during the process puts her in a position to ascend the next step, and so on. However, any weakness of skills at any step can result in a dangerous fall.

As children make subsequent attempts to climb stairs, they push themselves higher and higher out of their comfort zones. Doing so, they accumulate skills and mental representations of requisite movements and processes that enable them to safely do more than they could before.

Over time, teachers who deliberately practice most often acquire highly developed skills. They learn how to climb steps way beyond what they first envisioned.

Question # 37

Do You Have Common Sense?

Common sense is not so common.

—Voltaire

Teachers with common sense can navigate the daily trials and tribulations of a classroom, perceive what is happening around them, and make sound judgments and decisions. Their behavior is reasonable and typically unquestioned. They have skills to make connections and possess a common and reasonable sensibility.

You can check your own common sense by asking a respected teacher for feedback. As you reflect on his or her response, consider whether there was a delay before responding. The teacher might have been trying to think of a diplomatic way to answer the question honestly without hurting your feelings. The delay might be an indication that you have some work to do.

What can you be doing now to assure you have common sense?
1. Make sure you learn to make decisions based on fact.
2. Choose behaviors that enable you to live independently.
3. Develop basic cooking skills and understand nutrition.
4. Maintain good health and safety habits.
5. Recognize dangerous environments.
6. Demonstrate resourcefulness.
7. Develop a budget and live within your means.
8. Think and plan for yourself.
9. Develop relationships with people in your community.
10. Reflect with your mentor.

Developing common sense is a process, not a destination. Common sense is an outcome of being able to think things through for yourself, your students, their families, and your community.

Question # 38

What Is Your Emotional Intelligence Quotient?

All learning has an emotional base.

—Plato

Emotional intelligence (often abbreviated as EI or EQ) refers to the ability to perceive, control, and evaluate emotions. Teachers with better-than-average scores on emotional intelligence tend to be good at interpreting, understanding, and acting upon emotions. They are usually quite good at dealing with social or emotional conflicts, expressing their feelings, and dealing with emotional situations.

How would you respond to these statements?

	Strongly disagree	Disagree	Neutral	Agree	Strongly agree	No Opinion/ No Response
1. I am generally aware of how friends in my social circle feel.						
2. When upset, I can usually pinpoint why I am distressed.						
3. I generally like who I am.						
4. I feel uncomfortable in emotionally charged situations.						
5. I tend to avoid confrontations.						
6. I tend to overreact to minor problems.						
7. It takes me a while to really get to know a person.						

8. I feel confident about my own skills, talents, and abilities.						
9. I am a good judge of character.						
10. I tend to follow my instincts/intuition when making an important decision.						

The ability to manage emotions effectively is a crucial part of emotional intelligence. Teachers with a high EQ avoid allowing their emotions to influence choices related to high-risk actions.

Do you frequently have an emotional reaction to day-to-day events? Do you sometimes feel upset for no reason? Are you often in a bad mood? Has anyone ever referred to you as a 'drama queen'? If your answer is yes to any of these questions, you are experiencing some difficulties managing your emotions.

The key skills of emotional intelligence can be learned by anyone, at any time. When you experience an emotional situation, quickly reduce stressors. Respond by calming yourself down. Engage one or more of your senses: sight, sound, smell, taste, and touch. Each person responds differently to sensory input, so explore what most effectively helps calm you.

We can try to distort, deny, or numb our feelings, but we can't eliminate them. Without emotional awareness, we can quickly become overwhelmed. We are unable to fully understand our own motivations and needs and how to communicate effectively with others.

Humor, laughter, and play are natural antidotes to life's difficulties because they lighten burdens and help keep things in perspective. A good hearty laugh reduces stress, elevates mood, and brings your nervous system back into balance.

Just like learning to skillfully play the piano, EQ isn't something that can be started and then dropped. It requires a lifetime of practice, and it is always possible to improve. Even when you feel like you are on top of the world with a healthy EQ, keep practicing and you'll reap the benefits for the rest of your life.

According to *Psychology Today*, "Emotional intelligence is the ability to identify and manage your own emotions and the emotions of others."[17] This usually involves

- emotional awareness, which includes the ability to identify your own emotions as well as those of others.
- the ability to harness emotions and apply them to tasks such as problem solving.
- the ability to regulate your emotions, such as being able to calm down when you're upset.

17   https://www.psychologytoday.com/basics/emotional-intelligence

Question # 39

Are You Historically Literate and On Top of Current Events?

You've likely watched clips of late-night television hosts (such as Jay Leno, Jesse Watters, and Jimmy Fallon) interviewing random individuals on the street with questions you'd expect any educated person to be able to answer. The responses might make for good, lighthearted comedy, but laughing at someone's shortcomings is not a practice of effective teachers. However, if you don't know or are not able to recall basic historical facts, your students will laugh at you, and your reputation will suffer.

How well can you answer the questions in Table 9.2?

TABLE 9. 2 [18]

Question	Your Answer
1. How many British colonies declared independence in 1776 and can you name them?	
2. What year did Columbus discover the New World?	
3. In what decade did the American Civil War occur?	
4. Who was the first U.S. President?	
5. Who wrote the Declaration of Independence?	
6. Who wrote the Gettysburg Address?	
7. What important historical event occurred in these years? a) 1620 b) 1776 c) 1812 d) 1861 e) 1945 f) 2001	
8. What dictators did the U.S. help defeat during World War II?	

---

18 Answers can be found in the Appendix.

9. Who invented the light bulb?	
10. Who is called the King of Rock 'n' Roll?	

Teachers need to understand and be able to analyze chronological relationships, causes and effects of events, and differing historical perspectives. Additionally, teachers should be well grounded in their knowledge of key historical figures and geography.

As you prepare to teach, what can you do now? Read books about history. Pay close attention in history classes. Understand how a study of the past can affect what happens today and how ideas influence society. Learn your local community's history and facts about local historical figures and events.

Studying the past provides lessons for the present and guidance for the future. Likewise, you should be well informed about current events in your city, state, and the world. If not, how do you plan to respond when your students ask you questions about what is happening?

Just as it is important to be historically literate (regardless of your major), teachers must be knowledgeable and capable of conversing about business, politics, sports, arts, medicine, travel, popular culture, and world events. Learn to spot trends.

Watch news reports, read books and the newspaper, review trusted websites, and talk with informed people.

To become well informed, you must synthesize information from a variety of print and media sources. Pay attention as you watch the news (from all political angles), and engage in discussion with others about current events. Read the newspaper and listen to reliable podcasts. In particular, subscribe to education publications and specific interest or content-related journals (or find them in your school's library). Maintain a balance of reliable informative sources and points of view.

Recommended Reading:
Goldstein, Dana (2014). *The Teacher Wars: A History of America's Most Embattled Profession*. New York: Doubleday.

Question # 40

Can You Teach Using Current Technologies? Are You Digitally Savvy?

In the past two decades, there has been a strong push to get educational technology into the hands of teachers and students. Despite well-conceived plans and determined efforts, many obstacles to implementation still exist. These include equipment placed in inaccessible locations, hardware and software malfunctions, and a lack of technical support. However, the greatest obstacle may be that some teachers report lacking the time or motivation to learn technology skills.

Principals are seeking teachers of any age who can utilize technology in classrooms to improve student achievement. You will likely be asked during interviews about your abilities to teach using technology. Wise potential teachers take advantage of every opportunity to learn about multiple technologies, use them, and integrate them into their preparatory program.

Consider your personal technical skills. Can you type? Have you been taught proper keyboarding skills? Can you teach these skills to kids? If you can't respond positively to these questions, start today to work for high levels of personal proficiency.

Technology in a classroom includes computers, tablets, smartphones, presentation platforms, course management tools, collaboration tools, and more. We can't stress this enough: learn to teach with technology! Learn with your classmates. The best way to get ideas and inspiration is to learn with others.

Question # 41

Are You Informed About Key Aspects of School Law?

No man is above the law and no man is below it; nor do we ask any man's permission when we ask him to obey it. Obedience to the law is demanded as a right; not asked as a favor.

—Theodore Roosevelt

Textbooks used in teacher preparation programs commonly have at least one chapter devoted to school law. Your coursework should inform you about local, state, and federal legal systems, influential U.S. Supreme Court decisions, collective bargaining, school contracts, tenure, teacher and student rights, academic freedom, copyright laws, and much more.

As a student, and later as a beginning teacher, school law may not be a topic that sparks your interest. But with issues such as bullying, harassment, parent custody, child abuse, and personal and professional liability a constant concern and influence in teachers' lives, you need to be well informed in order to make decisions that are both legally sound and ethical.

A quick review of The National School Boards Association's website[19] includes news, resources issues and court decisions on a range of legal issues for public schools.

Equity and Discrimination (issues involving age, disability, race, ethnic origin, gender, and homeless status)

Employment (the major employment laws affecting schools)

Governance (legal and practical issues related to local school board control and how school boards operate)

Special Education and Disabilities (knowledge and compliance guidelines with federal laws such as the Individuals with Disabilities Education Act, § 504 of the Rehabilitation Act and the Americans with Disabilities Act)

Privatization and Choice (involving various reform measures, including public school choice, charter schools, privatization, vouchers, and alternative schools)

---

19   http://www.nsba.org/advocacy/school-law

Student Rights and Discipline (challenges school districts face in balancing students' First, Fourth, and Fifth Amendment rights with their educational mission to maintain a safe non-disruptive learning environment)

Athletics (Title IX, gender equity, student-athlete drug testing and codes of conduct, school district liability for sports-related injuries, and disabled students participation in interscholastic sports)

Curriculum (issues involving state and federal standards, teacher and student classroom speech, religious rights, and controversies over instruction, textbooks, and classroom and library materials)

Facilities (property issues including public land, facilities, and equipment, and control of property, purchasing procedure, eminent domain, and buildings and construction).

Health and Nutrition (resources on nutrition for student and employee health issues such as insurance, confidentiality of health records, health-related services, drugs, contagious diseases, and accommodations for health conditions)

Legal System (complying with constitutional, statutory, regulatory, and judicial legal requirements at the federal, state, and local levels)

Religion (issues related to the role of religion in the classroom, including First Amendment, Establishment, Free Exercise, and Free Speech clause issues)

School Safety (issues concerning student safety, school violence, student rights, harassment, and bullying)

Student Achievement (information on standardized tests, high-stakes testing, and academic honors)

Technology (issues related to the Internet, email, video, and other emerging technology)

A daunting list of issues and concerns? Without a doubt. However, it is important for you to learn about these if you want to have a long and successful career as a teacher. Add to that the many ethical decisions that teachers make each day, and you might think about reconsidering your decision to teach. Teachers who lose their jobs have usually acted irresponsibly in some way out of either negligence or ignorance.

Laws and professional codes of conduct serve as guidelines to help teachers make professional decisions. Unprofessional behavior and decisions can end your career. Know the law.

Question # 42

Do You Think You Can Teach and Be Politically Correct?

The greatest enemy of clear language is insincerity.

—George Orwell

Most teachers work in schools and live in communities that are multiethnic and multiracial. No one can hope to teach successfully while deliberately choosing to ignore race, class, or gender issues. Many people have become victims of intellectual and educational oppression since the founding of schools in the United States, often due to prejudice from ignorance. There is a heightened sense of political correctness in many public schools as they attempt to eliminate any remnant of racism, sexism, and class elitism and avoid discriminating against or offending students. However, political correctness can sometimes appear to conflict with principles of free speech, and can potentially leave a teacher in a tough spot.

Advocates of political correctness base their argument on a philosophy of inclusion and are concerned with correcting centuries of unfairness. At times, schools have silenced or removed teachers whose opinions differ from what is deemed politically correct. Conservatives and liberals view many issues differently, and teachers often find themselves trying to negotiate a middle ground between these two points of view.

So, how do aspiring teachers respect different points of view and remain aware of sensitive issues without compromising their own values and beliefs or becoming stigmatized for speaking their mind?

1. Self-assess your own prejudices. If you hold conscious or unconscious negative feelings or stereotypes towards individuals or groups, adjust your language and behavior.
2. Become well informed about prejudice in American society and the world. Learning about the struggles of people different from you can help you reevaluate your own preconceived notions.
3. Step outside of your comfort zone. Being politically correct also means learning about those different from you and respecting those differences.

4. In an inclusive classroom, familiarize yourself with politically correct terms for students with disabilities. Bullying, name-calling and other acts of verbal assault are often the result of ignorance. Teach students about disabilities, and promote tolerance and acceptance of others.
5. Ask questions. Talk with other teachers and your principals about the issues encompassed in a politically correct environment. Think before you speak or act.

The key to being politically correct is thinking and acting with respect. An intentional alteration of words or behavior to avoid either offending someone or reinforcing a disadvantageous stereotype is an indication of effective teaching.

Educational labels and terms constantly change. What is used or appears to be correct today may be outdated or offensive tomorrow. In an ever-changing world, teachers must ask how people choose to self-identify and be addressed. Do not assume that you know what someone wants to be called. Avoid labeling people according to stereotypes.

Question # 43

Are You Politically Active?

It had long since come to my attention that people of accomplishment rarely sat back and let things happen to them. They went out and happened to things.
—Leonardo da Vinci

When you become a teacher, you will likely become a member of a local, state and national teacher union. The influence and powers of public-sector unions, including teacher unions, have been a subject of contentious debate since they were formed. Regardless of your view of teacher unions, they will likely play an influential role in determining your contract and working conditions, as well as in educational reform. You can either watch from the sidelines or get involved and influence outcomes.

Decisions about educational reform are influenced by lobbyists and made by legislators in state capitals and Washington, D.C. Most often, those individuals haven't been in a classroom in a long while, if at all. You are the expert. You need to speak up for your profession, competently clarify your needs, express your professional viewpoint about what works and doesn't work with children and youth, and support your comments with data.

There is much to read and learn about teachers' political activism. Do not remain silent about issues that directly impact your work. Schools are political institutions. You need to be involved and have your voice heard.

However, while advocating your positions, keep in mind Aesop's fable about the boy that cried wolf. "To cry wolf" means to give a false alarm. Your voice will be more influential if you are discriminating about how and when you choose to speak up.

Recommended Reading
Goldstein, Dana (2014). *The Teacher Wars: A History of America's Most Embattled Profession.* New York: Doubleday.
Ravitch, Diane. *Reign of Error: The Hoax of the Privatization Movement and the Danger to America's Public Schools.* New York: Alfred A. Knopf.

CHAPTER 9

DISCUSSION QUESTIONS AND ACTIVITIES

1. Does your resume fully describe your level of preparation? What should you be doing each year of college to fully develop it? Work with a trusted professor or mentor to review it and plan how to fill gaps. Don't wait until you reach the end of your preparatory program to develop your resume.

2. Are you aware of the core competencies of social emotional learning (SEL)? The Collaborative for Academic, Social and Emotional Learning (CASEL) has identified five interrelated sets of cognitive, affective and behavioral competencies:
   - Self-awareness
   - Self-management
   - Social awareness
   - Relationship skills
   - Responsible decision making

3. Do you manage your emotions effectively? Teachers must be prepared to empathize, persevere, control impulses, communicate clearly, solve problems, and work with others. Follow the link and complete a self-assessment of your emotional intelligence. Discuss the results and feedback with trusted peers and colleagues.
   - Edutopia Quiz: What Is Your Emotional Intelligence (EQ)? http://www.edutopia.org/louisville-social-emotional-learning-quiz

4. Are you familiar with the term Executive Functioning? It is used to describe neurologically based skills involving mental control and self-regulation. Conduct an Internet research on this topic, become familiar with it, and discuss how it applies to the preparation and development of personal responsibility of teachers.

5. Conduct an Internet search of best education and/or classroom tech apps, explore their benefits, and share your findings with your peers.

CHAPTER 9 SELF-ASSESSMENT

HOW TO USE THIS ASSESSMENT GUIDE

Aspiring teachers are nurtured and supported through strong relationships. You should reflect privately, but you should also seek the perspective of and advice from teachers, professors, counselors, parents, friends, and others who can help you discern your personal and professional capacities as you prepare to become a teacher. There are no right answers. Be honest with yourself. When you are finished with this chapter, discuss your self-evaluation (see the chart below) with the people supporting you. Together, your self-evaluation and subsequent discussions should reveal strengths as well as areas for further growth.

If you frequently engage in reflective activities, you should be well prepared for any outcomes of formal evaluation practices.

My preparation and/or professional performance skills indicate that ...	Strongly disagree	Disagree	Neutral	Agree	Strongly agree	No Opinion/ No Response
36. I have an understanding of teaching career patterns, developmental stages, and advanced opportunities.						
37. I can effectively organize day-to-day events and activities.						
38. My EI and SEL levels are high.						

39. I am knowledgeable about important historical events and maintain an in-depth awareness of current events via the newspaper, TV news, and other media.					
40. I use technology effectively in the classroom and consider myself to be digitally savvy.					
41. I have studied the key court cases and laws impacting teaching and education.					
42. I am aware of cultural, political, and other sensitivities and feel capable of addressing them professionally.					
43. I am involved and capable of effectively speaking up to advocate for students and the teaching profession.					

CHAPTER 10

PERSONAL RESPONSIBILITY

You must accept personal responsibility for your preparation and performance as a teacher. No one else can do this for you.

Your mindset will determine the degree of personal responsibility others will see in you. It will also provide indicators into your understanding and acceptance of and adherence to professional thought, decorum, ethics, and commitment.

The questions in this chapter and throughout this book are intended to help you understand how the development of your personal mindset is the key determinant in your success or failure as a student, a professional, and a human being.

Find multiple ways to reflect, discuss, and plan strategies that showcase your personal responsibility. These skills will help you get and keep a job.

Question # 44

Can You Reliably Manage Time?

If you're ten minutes early you're on time, if you're five minutes early you're late.

—Vince Lombardi

Even a broken clock is right twice a day. This famous saying means that being minimally correct does not equate with reliability. Being reliable as a teacher means that others can consistently count on you to be present and accountable for your actions.

Reliability is an important character trait. Have you accumulated a proven track record?

Consider how reliability will impact your teaching. You will work with children and be the primary adult in charge of them. Their parents will rely on you to keep their children safe and secure. Being reliable means that you have to be consistent in fulfilling responsibilities. You can practice that consistency by being diligent about completing tasks that you are given in school.

It is best to build reliability by managing time in small steps. Learn to use a daily planner. Complete your homework. Turn it in on time. Read assignments. Consistently give your best effort at all times. Learn from mistakes. Be prompt to class and meetings. Earn others' trust.

For visual learners, post-it notes serve as effective reminder aides. Color-code your calendar to support the development of consistent and reliable habits. Add important information and dates in your smartphone calendar and set reminders for a week, a day, and hours before a task is to be completed.

Table 10.1 contains apps that are helpful in increasing organizational skills that create reliability. If you can't find the ones listed here, look for others that have similar functions.

Five Personal Apps to Help You Organize
Goggle Now organizes anything you can think of into cards that are customized to your needs.
24me is like a personal assistant who provides 24-hour reminders. The app syncs with your calendar and other apps and also allows you to share notes with friends or co-workers.
Quip allows you to collaborate with others on documents, spreadsheets, and checklists. Users can create, import or share documents as well as update them. There is a sidebar that allows you to check in with co-workers and review any edits.
Wunderlist allows you to organize your thoughts or activities. You are able to share lists with others and have conversations about them.
Speaktoit allows you to call, send texts, and search the web. You give it commands and it will give you the best selection or recommendations to fit your schedule.

Source: TechTimes.com (2015)

15 Rules for Building Reliability
1. Keep your promises.
2. Don't overpromise.
3. Don't leave other people hanging.
4. Whatever you do, do it well.
5. Be consistent.
6. Finish what you start.
7. Pull your weight and shoulder your own responsibilities.
8. Manage expectations.
9. Be honest.
10. Be punctual.
11. Be fair and consistent in rewards and punishments.
12. Don't let circumstances dictate your behavior.
13. Don't collapse in emergencies.
14. Show up.
15. Learn to say no.

Question # 45

Do You Mind Your Own Business?

To mind your own business incorporates the whole duty of man.
—Brigham Young

When you look in the mirror, do you ever see a busybody, someone who meddles in others' affairs or spreads gossip and starts rumors?

Minding one's own business and staying out of others' affairs is generally good advice. However, aspiring and beginning teachers need to be careful to find a balance between minding their own business and inappropriate actions like closing the door to their classroom, staying to themselves, failing to collaborate, and avoiding social activities.

Community is important for everyone, but it especially so for educators because teaching can be a lonely profession. The age difference between students and teachers is often wide. Even at the high school or college level, where age differences may be less, it helps for teachers to be able to communicate with their peers and belong to a professional learning community.

Well-adjusted teachers with high EQ (see Question 38) understand the need for community. They belong to and commune with faith-based groups, participate in civic service organizations, join clubs, volunteer, socialize with friends, and enjoy support and encouragement to teach. They play active roles in their professional associations. They understand the importance of building and sustaining a professional network. As a result, they report to being happier, healthier, safer, and less likely to suffer from stress, isolation, and despair at work. They consider their teaching partners to be their friends as much as their colleagues.

Obviously, what you do with your life is ultimately your business. However, teachers should not engage in dangerous or unprofessional activities. Your participation in such activities can potentially isolate you because other teachers may not want to be associated with you.

Ultimately, you should get involved in your professional community. Your resume should reflect

- membership in your student education association.
- high school and collegiate extracurricular activities.

155

- examples of your ability to be a team player.
- patterns of collaboration.
- models of compassion and service to others.

Who in your life can hold up a mirror and show you who you really are? Do you see yourself as part of a community of learners, or do you choose to play a solo act?

The pioneers involved in this country's westward expansion had to become industrious and ingenious, and they had to know how to cope with loneliness and dangers, such as severe weather and conflicts with Native Americans. To survive, they established communities, connected with and protected one another, shared resources, and created happier and healthier lives amidst the vast, sparsely settled lands of the Great Plains. They minded their own business, but clearly saw the need, as well as the power and safety, of community.

Researchers have used the term **Professional Learning Community (PLC)** since the 1960s. Rick DuFour and his colleagues helped clarify the concept and the potential of PLCs in educational settings in the 1990s. Today, a PLC might broadly describe any gathering of individuals who share a common interest in education. Professional learning communities operate under the assumption that the key to higher student achievement is continuous job-embedded learning for educators.

Question # 46

Do You Have Any "Pre-existing" Conditions?

This question differs from a previous one about criminal background checks. It pertains to behaviors or untreated psychological conditions that would likely disqualify you from teaching if left unchanged or untreated. What are some of these pre-existing conditions?

- You have expressed racist or sexist views.
- You had an addiction (to drugs, alcohol, porn, sex, etc.).
- You lied or cheated compulsively.
- You have been self-centered. (Your needs always came first.)
- You have been hypocritical. (You believed rules, expectations, or high standards that apply to others don't apply to you.)
- You had a severe, untreated psychological condition that caused you to act impulsively or inappropriately or affected your ability to have healthy interactions with others.

Past behaviors have a way of coming back to haunt. It is important for aspiring teachers to consider the seriousness of their past actions and the potential negative consequences on their professional career should old behaviors re-emerge. If you are still struggling to stop unethical or dangerous behaviors, you should get help and consider delaying your educational career until you can appropriately modify them.

Teachers encounter many people, including parents of their students, who act in inappropriate ways and create havoc in their children's lives. Children struggle to develop in healthy ways when their parents have untreated addictions, mental health issues, or other challenging conditions, and in these cases, it is even more important that teachers take care of themselves and act professionally and ethically. Helping children overcome extremely challenging home lives may be one of your job requirements.

Consistently behaving with integrity and attending to any conditions that need to be treated is why teachers need a gritty growth mindset. Those who possess that outlook know that intelligence, personality, and character are shaped and developed throughout a lifetime. Teachers with growth mindsets are determined to succeed, overcome challenges, learn from mistakes, adopt and maintain good habits, and put forth tremendous amounts of sustained effort over long periods of time to achieve goals. No matter what burdens they might have carried in their past, they possess a gritty determination and commitment to live in the present and never to return to the error of their ways.

During job interviews, it is fair to be asked if you have any pre-existing conditions or past behaviors that would prevent you from fulfilling the responsibilities listed in a job description. If you do, talk with your mentor. Should you decide to openly share your pre-existing conditions or past behaviors, you must do so in ways that convince listeners that you are now progressing with habits of a growth mindset.

Your teacher shadow can hover for a lifetime. Make sure that shadow is free of any blotches or stains.

Question # 47

Do You Have Eyes in the Back of Your Head?

Never lie to a mom, she always finds out.

—Every Mom

Do you remember when you first thought your mom seemed to have eyes in the back of her head? Some people also call that skill, which is possessed by most mothers and teachers, as with-it-ness.

Teachers must possess an ability to "read" a room. They must be able to see everything at all times, even when their backs are facing the students. They must possess keen senses of smell and hearing.

You've likely watched a television crime show in which a reporter tells a story from different people's perspective. Even though the same event was witnessed, people see things differently and recall different facts. The person who is best able to scan and notice minute, specific details, is considered the most reliable.

Teacher "radar" is another way to describe with-it-ness. Teachers become alarmed when normal noise levels suddenly change. Their radar senses trouble when students' body language doesn't match expectations. Part of effective classroom management skills, this radar constantly scans for good and bad behavior. Effective teachers have the flexibility to respond when needed by changing pace, moving about the room, and interacting with students to redirect and refocus.

What can you do to develop your teacher radar? Observe how experts manage small details. Those who routinely gloss over the small details miss the bigger picture.

Think about the *Highlights* magazine you might have seen in a doctor's office.[20] Remember the picture search puzzles? They challenged you to look for specific shapes or objects within a larger picture. At first, you probably didn't see all the smaller items because you were looking at the larger picture. But, after examining more closely, you learned to pick out the objects you were searching for and developed a sense of how small things can be connected to larger pictures.

---

20   https://www.highlights.com/

What can aspiring teachers do to improve their radar? Follow these tips.

- Become aware of multiple senses—notice the random sounds in the classroom, the voices of students, smells, people walking past the classroom door—while you are in class or while you conduct a lesson.
- Practice looking around classrooms—a teacher who has with-it-ness seems to have x-ray vision.
- Practice maintaining composure while dealing with the demands of several peers or students at the same time.
- Develop the ability to stop misconduct with a look.
- Learn the "ripple effect"—correcting one student's misbehavior will positively influence the behavior of other nearby students.

"With-it-ness" is a term created by Jacob Kounin to describe the teacher's awareness of what is going on in all parts of the classroom at the same time. Can you meet the demands of several students at the same time? Do you know how to adjust a lesson's momentum by changing activities when interest is waning or modifying activities to keep students busy? With-it-ness increases student involvement and minimizes misbehavior.

Question # 48

Have You Been Weaned? Are You an Adult?

Your mother can't go to your job interviews. Nor should your father keep a constant eye on you while you work in your first classroom. Parents can't forever shield you from the real world.

Baby Boomer parents are being credited with developing a parenting philosophy that was soft on discipline and heavy on spoiling their children. The Generation X parents are becoming even more notorious for coddling their kids. As a result, college admissions officers and professors are experiencing increasing numbers of students whose parents are exerting control over students' academic work, extracurricular activities, and career choices. Julie Lythcott-Haims, former dean of freshman at Stanford University, wrote in her manifesto against helicopter parenting, *How to Raise an Adult*, that many of the students she worked with from hyper-attentive parents were poorly equipped to handle the demands and challenges of college.

"Helicopter parenting" is a term that's been in use for nearly 50 years, first in 1969 by Dr. Haim Ginott, an Israeli teacher, child psychologist, and parent educator. In contrast, "Free-Range Parenting," which is used by author Lenore Skenazy in her 2009 book *Free-Range Kids: Giving Our Children the Freedom We Had Without Going Nuts with Worry*, describes the self-confidence, happiness, and self-sufficiency that comes from allowing kids to do some things on their own. Not without controversy, free-range parenting is limited by state laws, which prohibit children from wandering alone. Despite the extremes in these approaches to child rearing, many parents produce children who become well-adjusted adults.

Obviously, there is a delicate balance between nurturing and independence and between protective and overinvolved parenting. No one would wish for anything less than all children having parents who love them fiercely. But by the time you are in college, your mother needs to stop editing your papers and calling professors to question their judgment or authority. Parents shouldn't be playing the role of concierge for adults in college.

By the end of high school, students must be able to talk to new people, handle problems with friends, live alone and manage a household; manage assignments, workload, and deadlines; assess and take risks; earn and manage money; and cope with the challenges of having tough college professors or bosses. College students who are successful in an increasingly competitive world learn to work and problem-solve independently without parental interference.

Every child needs parents to "be there" but also know when and where to appropriately draw lines. Parent over-involvement in the minutiae of teaching and grading impacts the practice of education.

Reflect on your upbringing and that of your peers. Do you think you can handle the challenges of teaching without your parents' influence? If you have any doubts or concerns, consult with your teachers or a mentor and develop a plan to increase your independence.

Author Tim Elmore, in his book *Generation iY: Our Last Chance to Save Them*, lists seven lies told to the iY Generation (born mostly in the 80s and 90s) that he believes have caused many Millennials to reach adulthood emotionally unstable and socially naïve.

1. You can be anything you want to be.
2. It's your choice.
3. You are special.
4. Everyone should go to college.
5. You can have it now.
6. You're a winner because you participated.
7. You can have/get whatever you want.

Do you aspire to be a supportive teacher or a demanding teacher? Will you firmly enforce expectations with authoritarian tough love, or will you strive to motivate students more through permissive support and affection? In her book *Grit: The Power of Passion and Perseverance*,[1] psychologist Angela Duckworth suggests that parents and teachers can wisely utilize both strategies.[2] Table 10.1 provides a visualization of wise parenting (a.k.a teaching).

---

1   Adapted from p. 212, *Grit: The Power of Passion and Perseverance*
2   Table 10.1 is also modified from the work on parenting styles by Diana Baumrind
http://www.positive-parenting-ally.com/3-parenting-styles.html

TABLE 10.1

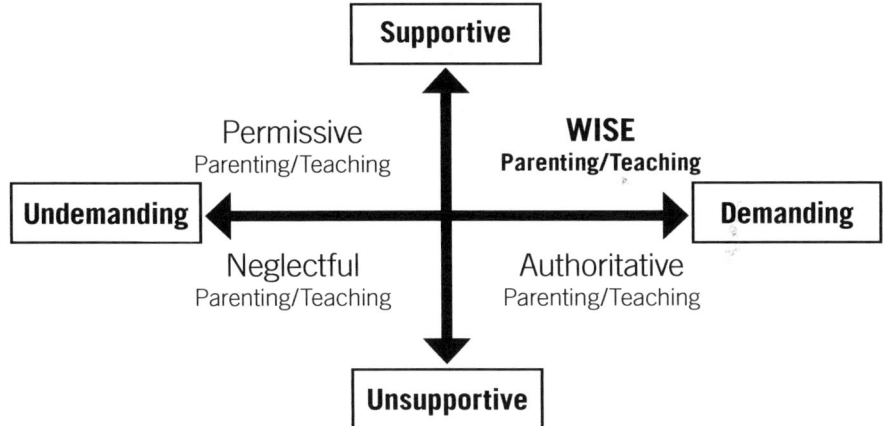

Question # 49

Do You Understand the Concept of Diversity?

Strength lies in differences, not in similarities.

—Stephen Covey

The news and social media contain countless stories about diversity. But what exactly is meant by diversity? How would you respond in a job interview if asked a question such as, "What does diversity mean to you and how might it look in your classroom?"

Most people think diversity pertains to race, but it's more than that. Diversity relates to anything that makes people different. It encompasses class, ethnicity, gender, socioeconomic status, learning abilities, physical abilities, and religion. Multiculturalism concerns the understanding and acceptance of ethnic cultures, while diversity deals with a wider range of identity categories that includes ethnic cultures. Every student is unique, and every classroom is diverse. Diversity makes us stronger, and it does not need to create adversity.

How are you unique? In what ways are you different from others? Do you view people as individuals, with unique needs and desires, or do you observe people in broad groups? Teachers need to develop classrooms that support a broad range of ideas and initiatives that create safe, inclusive learning environments with equitable opportunities for a diverse group of students.

It is important to create a "diversity lens" in order to effectively examine individual needs in different ways. Scrutinizing your own bias is a great way to start. Everyone has biases. Sports fans have a bias for their favorite team, music lovers for their favorite performers. But bias can become problematic when it manifests as prejudice or discrimination. If you have a tendency to prejudge or discriminate, educate yourself about how to eliminate these behaviors. It is a teacher's responsibility to create a positive educational environment for *all* people.

A good way to experience and understand diversity is to travel. Learn about the norms and customs of other people. Discover how to effectively interact with people who are different from you. Travel to other cities, states, and countries. Experience different foods, transportation systems, shopping, museums, parks, faith-based groups, and housing.

Obtaining a global perspective can also provide insights into how to relate to the experience of others. Misunderstandings often occur when people do not understand each other's belief systems or ideas. Teachers must comprehend and teach facts about diversity.

What can an aspiring teacher do to expand the concept of diversity?
- Read. Expand your knowledge base of the world beyond your hometown.
- Learn about key U.S. Supreme Court cases that have shaped issues related to diversity in education.
- Experience college and community ethnic fairs.
- Explore and become familiar with books and resources pertaining to diversity in your school's library.
- Understand differing lifestyles (e.g., rural vs. urban, religious, ethnic).
- Read about or take courses focused on issues of globalization.
- Watch movies that address issues of diversity.
- Utilize television's *History Channel* and other media resources.
- Identify community-based speakers that can complement your lessons and bring relevancy to student learning.
- Develop teaching strategies and methods that are inclusive rather than exclusive.

Listed below are titles of movies and books about issues related to diversity. Watch or read them and explore whether they'd be appropriate to use in your future classrooms.

Movies	Books
Whale Rider (2002)	*Three Cups of Tea* by Greg Mortenson and David Oliver Relin
Tortilla Soup (2001)	*The Color Purple* by Alice Walker
Eat, Pray, Love (2010)	*Unbroken* by Laura Hillenbrand
Marco Polo (2007)	*127 Hours* by Aron Ralston
Seven Years in Tibet (1997)	*Soul Surfer* by Bethany Hamilton
Hotel Rwanda (2005)	*The Kite Runner* by Khaled Hosseini

Boys Don't Cry (2005)	*The Help* by Kathryn Stockett
Amistad (2005)	*Roll of Thunder, Hear My Cry* by Mildred D. Taylor
Mississippi Burning (1988)	*Copper Sun* by Sharon M. Draper
Akeelah and the Bee (2006)	*Some of My Best Friends Are Black* by Tanner Colby
Billy Elliot (2000)	*To Kill a Mockingbird* by Harper Lee
Remember the Titans (2006)	*He Named me Malala* by Malala Yousafzai

Question # 50

Can You Showcase Your Passion?

Hire for passion first, experience second and credentials third.
—Paul Alofs, author of *Passion Capital*

Many young people say that they have a passion for music. They mean they have a strong or extravagant fondness, enthusiasm, or sustainable desire for anything related to a favorite genre of music.

If there's one quality that principals report that they look for during interviews, it is passion. In fact, above and beyond the many characteristics we've described in this book, principals seek teachers with a sincere, sustainable passion for learning, for teaching, growing, and most importantly, working with kids. Do you have a sustainable passion for teaching? Or would some describe your passion as a huge burst of enthusiasm that is quick to diminish when things get tough?

Many aspiring teachers appear to be naturally passionate about everything they do. Others have a style that can be difficult to perceive and understand. A few are obviously dispassionate and should not become teachers. Are you capable of self-monitoring your passion?

How can you be certain that others see your passion for teaching?
1. Make sure your body language conveys energy and enthusiasm. That is difficult to do if you don't routinely exercise, get plenty of rest, and prepare yourself mentally and physically for the rigors of teaching.
2. Share a variety of stories that easily illustrate points about your teaching experience, interests, and strengths. Stories make abstract concepts more relative, understandable, and memorable. When you talk about yourself, observers should hear and see your passion.
3. Use gestures and move around effectively to accentuate points when you talk. But guard against talking too much with your hands.
4. Maintain eye contact with all of your listeners. Allow your passion to shine from within you. Avoid anything that would make your

167

eyes look tired or appear a reddish color (e.g., allergies, excessive drinking, smoking, lack of sleep, etc.)

5. Smile when you speak. Share your joy and pleasure. People will perceive your passion most when you smile.

6. Avoid verbal graffiti, fillers such as *um* and *like*, that will distract your message.

7. Passionate speakers utilize differing vocal rates, dynamics (syntax and sentence structure), volume, and tone for effect. A slower rate is used for emphasis, while a faster rate expresses energy and excitement. Dynamics are used for contrasts and create interest. Make sure sentences don't follow the same structure, and ensure you don't raise or lower your tone inappropriately at the end of sentences. Speak at a moderate volume most of the time. Make sure people can hear you, but do not shout. Vary your tone to express feelings—a consistent tone, or monotone, is boring.

8. Dress appropriately. Your passion for teaching might be perceived as fake if you don't look the part.

9. Express your personal ideas and feelings. Think for yourself. Avoid scripted statements and clichés that everyone has heard numerous times and prefers not to hear again.

10. Most importantly, talk about your love for kids and the importance of their learning. You should say 'us' or 'them' much more often than you say 'me.'

CHAPTER 10

DISCUSSION QUESTIONS

1. Do you procrastinate? Are you often in a rush to complete assignments? Do you have a hard time juggling school, work, and personal time? Share your ideas about the successful time management strategies listed below with your teachers, mentors, and peers:
   - Develop a daily schedule in fifteen-minute increments. List everything—meals, rest, travel time, etc. (See notes at the end of this book for a scheduling template.)
   - Make a to-do list, and prioritize by identifying the most important tasks to complete.
   - Establish specific goals and times to complete work.
   - Identify times between classes and work schedules that can be better used to accomplish what is most needed.

2. What factors are motivating you to become a teacher? How do you define and demonstrate passion? Think about these and then share your thoughts with others.

3. Part of developing personal responsibility is becoming aware and comfortable with who you really are. Explain how you will respond to this question assessing your responsibility in an interview:

What are three of your strengths and three of your weaknesses?

Strengths	Strengths Rationale	Weaknesses	Weaknesses Rationale
1.		1.	
2.		2.	
3.		3.	

Develop a plan showing strategies to improve in both areas.

CHAPTER 10 SELF-ASSESSMENT

HOW TO USE THIS ASSESSMENT GUIDE

Aspiring teachers are nurtured and supported through strong relationships. You should reflect privately, but you should also seek the perspective of and advice from teachers, professors, counselors, parents, friends, and others who can help you discern your personal and professional capacities as you prepare to become a teacher. There are no right answers. Be honest with yourself. When you are finished with this chapter, discuss your self-evaluation (see the chart below) with the people supporting you. Together, your self-evaluation and subsequent discussions should reveal strengths as well as areas for further growth.

If you frequently engage in reflective activities, you should be well prepared for any outcomes of formal evaluation practices.

My preparation and/or professional performance skills indicate that...	Strongly disagree	Disagree	Neutral	Agree	Strongly agree	No Opinion/ No Response
44. I can be counted on to routinely and punctually fulfill commitments.						
45. I belong to and play an active role in my professional learning community and professional associations.						
46. I am aware of my actions and those of students in the classroom.						

47. I do not have any "skeletons in the closet" that would impact my ability to teach.						
48. I am supported appropriately by my parents and family. I act in the mature manner expected of a young adult.						
49. I am informed and sensitive to diversity issues.						
50. Others easily perceive that I am passionate about teaching.						

SUMMARY

So you think you can teach? After reading the questions we've presented in this book, we hope that you will reflect on this question with a growth mindset, ask questions, discuss your reactions, share opinions, and develop plans for reaching your potential as an effective teacher. Ultimately, we want readers to realize that they can teach, that they like teaching, that it fulfills them each day, and that the attainment of the character skills we've outlined requires a lifetime of gritty persistence to fully develop.

Teacher preparation is a process that spans a career, not just the time spent in college. Our work as professors is to help students discern whether teaching is a good career choice, teach academic content and pedagogy, equip aspirants with grit skills, and within a short amount of time, enable them to develop a growth mindset philosophy that will support a successful transition to the trials and rigors of the "real" classroom. Then, as their career unfolds, we expect principals, teacher leaders, and mentors to continue providing instruction and support. With circular communication between teacher preparation programs and receiving schools, we can continue to improve how new teachers perceive and deliver content, and also how they deploy the skills needed to make connections and build relationships with both students and adults.

All professional societies share common understandings of desirable character skills and codes of conduct that differentiate 'right' and 'wrong' decision making. Ethical codes guide practice for individual employees, as well as an entire organization. Many of the questions presented in this book are focused on ethical principles, but they serve more as an outline of skills that good teachers know and utilize to do their jobs. In our attempt to raise important questions, identify critical issues, imply a standard of skill development, we do not suggest that all teachers look the same. Some of the best teachers have unique, endearing personality traits that help them build relationships and connect with kids in ways that no one else can. Their differences make them special—and effective.

We hope our work reinforces your passion for teaching, encourages you to join and commit to a noble profession, and helps you become a very special person in the life of each of your students. Let us know what you think. Share your stories with us. Let us help you address concerns. Follow us and connect through Twitter, Facebook, or LinkedIn or via email at our university at https://www.ohio.edu/lancaster/. Let's grow, together!

APPENDIX

Answers for questions in table 9.2

Question	Answers
11. How many British colonies declared independence in 1776 and can you name them?	How many? 13 MA, NH, CT, RI, NY, PA, NJ, DE, MD, VA, NC, SC, GA
12. What year did Columbus discover the New World?	1492
13. In what decade did the American Civil War occur?	1860s
14. Who was the first U.S. President?	George Washington
15. Who wrote the Declaration of Independence?	Thomas Jefferson
16. Who wrote the Gettysburg Address?	Abraham Lincoln
17. What important historical event occurred in these years?	
a) 1620	a) 1620 Pilgrims land at Plymouth Rock
b) 1776	b) 1776 Declaration of Independence
c) 1812	c) 1812 War of 1812
d) 1861	d) 1861 U.S. Civil War began
e) 1945	e) 1945 World War II ended.
f) 2001	f) 2001 9-11 attacks on the US
18. What dictators did the U.S. help defeat during World War II?	Adolph Hitler of Germany Benito Mussolini of Italy
19. Who invented the light bulb?	Thomas Edison
20. Who is called the King of Rock n' Roll?	Elvis Presley

From Discussion Questions, Chapter 10

	Monday	Tuesday	Wednesday	Thursday	Friday	Saturday	Sunday
My Weekly Schedule							
7:00 a.m.							
8:00							
8:30							
9:00							
9:30							
10:00							
10:30							
11:00							
11:30							
12:00 p.m.							
12:30							
1:00							
1:30							
2:00							
2:30							
3:00							
3:30							
4:00							
4:30							
5:00							
5:30							
6:00 p.m.							
6:30							
7:00							
8:00							
9:00							
10:00							
11:00							

Sample Likert Scale					
First Impressions: Nonverbal aspects of interviewing	Strongly disagree	Somewhat disagree	Neither agree nor disagree	Somewhat agree	Strongly agree
1. Competent	1	2	3	4	5
2. Confident	1	2	3	4	5
3. Enthusiastic	1	2	3	4	5
4. Honest	1	2	3	4	5
5. Likable	1	2	3	4	5
6. (Not Anxious)	1	2	3	4	5
7. Professional	1	2	3	4	5
8. Warm	1	2	3	4	5
9. Positive	1	2	3	4	5
10. Passionate	1	2	3	4	5

References and Recommended Readings

Brafman, Ori, and Brafman, Rom. (2010). *Click: The Magic of Instant Connections*. New York: Broadway Books.

Burgess, Dave (2012). *Teach Like a Pirate*. San Diego: Dave Burgess Consulting, Inc.

Chester, Eric. (2012). *Reviving Work Ethic: A Leader's Guide to Ending Entitlement and Restoring Pride in the Emerging Workforce*. Austin, TX: Greenleaf Book Group Press.

Chua, Amy & Rubenfeld, Jed (2014). *The Triple Package: How Three Unlikely Traits Explain the Rise and Fall of Cultural Groups in America*. New York: Penguin Press.

Coats, C. (1994). *Things Your Mother Always Told You but You Didn't Want to Hear*. Nashville: Thomas Nelson Publishers.

Colvin, Geoff (2008). *Talent Is Overrated: What Really Separates World-Class Performers from Everybody Else*. New York: Penguin Group.

Crenshaw, Dave (2008). *The Myth of Multitasking: How "Doing It All" Gets Nothing Done*. San Francisco: Jossey-Bass.

Davis, Vicki (2014). *True Grit: The Best Measure of Success and How to Teach It*. Edutopia, January 9, 2014.

Duckworth, Angela. Google 12- Item Grit Scale. https://upenn.app.box.com/s/et30heyb2e7keq4t2w8b7c651230pscn

Duhigg, Charles (2012). *The Power of Habit: Why We Do What We Do in Life and Business*. New York: Random House.

Dweck, Carol (2007). *Mindset: The New Psychology of Success*. New York: Random House.

Elmore, Tim (2012). *Artificial Maturity: Helping Kids Meet The Challenge of Becoming Authentic Adults*. San Francisco: Jossey-Bass.

Elmore, Tim (2010). *Generation iY: Our Last Chance to Save Their Future*. Atlanta: Poet Gardener Publishing.

Elmore, Tim (2014). *12 Huge Mistakes Parents Can Avoid: Leading Your Kids to Succeed in Life*. Eugene, OR: Harvest House Press.

Farber, Katy. (2010). *Why Great Teachers Quit and How We Might Stop the Exodus*. Thousand Oaks, CA: Corwin Press.

Gardner, Margo, Roth, and Brooks-Gunn, Jeanne. (2008). Adolescents Participation in Organized Activities and Developmental Success

2 and 8 Years After High School: Do Sponsorship, Duration, and Intensity Matter? *Developmental Psychology* 44, 814-30.

Gladwell, Malcolm (2008). *Outliers: The Story of Success.* New York: Little, Brown & Company.

Gladwell, Malcolm (2013). *David and Goliath: Underdogs, Misfits, and the Art of Battling Giants.* New York: Little, Brown & Company.

Goldstein, Dana (2014). *The Teacher Wars: A History of America's Most Embattled Profession.* New York: Doubleday.

Gorksi, Paul (2013). *Reaching and Teaching Students in Poverty: Strategies for Erasing the Opportunity Gap.* New York: Teachers College Press.

Greitens, E. (2015). *Resilience.* New York: Harcourt, Houghton, Mifflin.

Hoerr, Thomas R. (2013). *Fostering Grit: How Do I Prepare My Students for The Real World?* Alexandria, VA: ASCD.

Jensen, Eric (2013). *Engaging Students with Poverty in Mind: Practical Strategies for Raising Achievement.* Alexandria, VA: ASCD.

Ingersoll, R. (2012). Beginning Teacher Induction: What the Data Tell Us. *Phi Delta Kappan,* Vol. 93, No. 8, p. 47–51.

Kirschner, Rick. (2011). *How to Click with People: The Secret to Better Relationships in Business and in Life.* New York: Hyperion.

Kohn, Alfie (2014). *The Myth of the Spoiled Child: Challenging the Conventional Wisdom about Children and Parenting.* Boston: Da Capo Press.

Lythcott-Haims, Julie (2015). *How to Raise an Adult: Break Free of the Overparenting Trap and Prepare Your Kid for Success.* New York: Henry Holt and Company.

Maxwell, John (2002). Leadership 101: *What Every Leader Needs to Know. Nashville:* Thomas Nelson Publishers.

Maxwell, John (2003). Relationships 101: *What Every Leader Needs to Know.* Nashville: Thomas Nelson Publishers.

Maxwell, John (2008). Mentoring 101: *What Every Leader Needs to Know.* Nashville: Thomas Nelson Publishers.

Meyer, Urban. (2015). *Above the Line: Lessons in Leadership and Life from a Championship Season.* New York: Penguin Random House.

Pappano, Laura (2013). *"Grit" and the New Character Education.* Harvard Education Newsletter Vol. 29, Number 1—Jan./Feb.

Ravitch, Diane. Reign of Error: *The Hoax of the Privatization Movement and the Danger to America's Public Schools*. New York: Alfred A. Knopf.

Reeves, D. & Allison, E. (2009). *Renewal Coaching: Sustainable Change for Individuals and Organizations*. San Francisco: Jossey-Bass.

Ricci, Mary Cay (2013). *Mindsets in the Classroom: Building a Culture of Success and Student Achievement in Schools*. Waco, TX: Purfrock Press, Inc.

Roberts, Yvonne (2009). *Grit. The Skills for Success and How They Are Grown*. London: Young Foundation

Robinson, Ken (2015). *Creative Schools. The Grassroots Revolution That's Transforming Schools*. New York: Viking/Penguin Publishing Group.

Seligman, Martin E. P. (2011). *Flourish: A Visionary New Understanding of Happiness and Well-being*. New York: Atria Paperback/Simon & Shuster, Inc.

Silver, Debbie (2012). *Fall Down 7 Times, Get Up 8*. Teaching Kids to Succeed. Thousand Oaks, CA; Corwin Press.

Skenazy, Lenore (2009). *Free-Range Kids: Giving Our Children the Freedom We Had Without Going Nuts with Worry*. San Francisco: Jossey-Bass.

Stoltz, Paul (2014). *Grit: The New Science of What It Takes to Persevere, Flourish, and Succeed*. Climb Strong Press (www.climbstrongpress.com)

Thaler, Linda Kaplan and Koval, Robin (2015). *Grit to Great: How Perseverance, Passion, and Pluck Take You from Ordinary to Extraordinary*. New York: Random House.

Tough, Paul (2012). *How Children Succeed: Grit, Curiosity, and the Hidden Power of Character*. Boston: Houghton Mifflin Harcourt.

Tulgan, Bruce (2009). *Not Everyone Gets a Trophy: How to Manage Generation Y*. San Francisco: Jossey-Bass.

Whitaker, Todd, Whitaker, Madeline, & Whitaker, Katherine (2016). *Your First Year: How to Survive and Thrive as a New Teacher*. New York: Routledge; Taylor and Francis Group.

Wormeli, Rick. Perseverance and Grit. *AMLE Magazine*, Jan. 2014, Vol. 1, #5

ABOUT THE AUTHORS

Paul G. Young, Ph.D., has worked as a high school band director, elementary and junior high classroom teacher (grades 4, 5, and 7), an elementary school principal, and executive director of an afterschool program director during a 40 year+ professional career in the Lancaster, Ohio, area. Additionally, for more than 30 years he has served as an adjunct professor of music and education classes at Ohio University-Lancaster Campus.

He served in leadership roles with both the National Association of Elementary School Principals (NAESP) and the National AfterSchool Association (NAA). He served as president of the 30,000 member NAESP in 2002–2003. He served as a member of the NAA Board of Directors starting in 2008 before becoming NAA's President and CEO in 2010. He retired from association work in 2012. He has written extensively on the topic of school and afterschool alignment, led training workshops throughout the country, and played an influential role in the development of practical, evidence-based alignment strategies for school leaders and afterschool professionals. He is the author of *Principal Matters: 101 Tips for Creating Collaborative Relationships Between After-School Programs and School Leaders* available at www.ExtendEDcotes.com. He is also an administrative columnist for EducationWorld.com at http://www.educationworld.com/a_admin/columnists/young/index.shtml.

Terri Green, M.A., has a Bachelor of Science Degree in Education from Bowling Green State University and a master degree from The Ohio State University in Literature, Language, and Reading. While employed by the Lancaster City Schools, she was a learning disabilities teacher, Reading Recovery and library resource teacher, and district literacy coordinator. Presently, she teaches the literacy courses as part of the early and middle childhood licensure programs offered at Ohio University-Lancaster. She serves as faculty advisor for the Ohio Student Education Association at OU-L, which supports aspiring teachers by offering them opportunities to gain personal growth and professional competence. Terri has been videotaped by the Literacy Specialist Project and the Ohio Department of Education for a professional development video series. Recently, she was a co-grant writer (with Lancaster City Schools) and winner of an Ohio Department of Education Third Grade Reading Grant. Through partnerships with area educators, she believes both pre-service and in-service teachers and their P–12 students can experience many mutual benefits. OU-L's weekly Lunch and Learn Seminar Series ("So You Think You Can Teach") and the success of the Ohio Student Education Association at Ohio University-Lancaster are outcomes of this belief.

Debra Dunning, Ph.D., is an Early Childhood and Child Development instructor at Ohio University-Lancaster. She has a Bachelor of Science degree from Bowling Green State University in Education and a master degree and doctorate degree from The Ohio State University in Human Ecology. Dr. Dunning previously taught at The Ohio State University and Ashland University. Her teaching includes working with preschool- and kindergarten-age children in both profit and non-profit daycare centers. She has also served as a program director, assistant director, and director of childcare centers. Dr. Dunning is a speaker in the community on a variety of topics including kindergarten readiness, developmentally appropriate practice, and parenting practices. Dr. Dunning has traveled to Zimbabwe, Africa, for missionary trips to aid children and families in a remote village. She tells their stories of grit, persistence, and inspiration to encourage others.

ABOUT LUNCH AND LEARN SEMINARS ("SO YOU THINK YOU CAN TEACH?")

Is it better to be a big fish in a small pond or a small fish in a big pond? We feel that for the preparation of aspiring teachers, it is better to be the big fish in a small pond.

Our regional campus is a small pond. But regardless of its size, our students, like most others, need individualized attention, support, and close relationships with their professors. They need multiple opportunities to focus on the development of the essential soft character skills described in this book. They need to see and experience practical examples of grit and growth mindset and receive continuous encouragement. They need "big fish" opportunities and experiences to complete tasks with others and to achieve shared goals in environments not as easily found in larger, perhaps more impersonal settings. Learning to collaborate, and to demonstrate the capacity to do it well, is an important resume objective.

To address our students' needs, we developed weekly, voluntary Lunch and Learn Seminars that provide our education majors with opportunities to become big fish—to learn, showcase their initiative, practice leadership, develop speaking and listening skills, ask questions, and develop contacts and relationships within the campus and community (to foster a professional learning community). We actively invite school administrators, teachers, and recent graduates in our area to share their expertise, professionalism, and "real world" experiences and practices. Despite scheduling challenges, participant feedback has been overwhelmingly positive. The relationships developed from these weekly gatherings have increased the visibility and confidence of, as well as the respect for, our graduating seniors. As a result, our graduates have been hired in many area school districts.

Our focus on establishing circular communications with our customers (area schools where our students obtain most jobs) has better informed us about what those customers want in new teachers and compelled us to share that awareness in our classes. In order to plan the weekly learning opportunities, we've met more frequently and listened more intently to our students as they've talked about their experience at our campus. We've become better collaborators, we've shared ideas, and as a result, we've become better professors. And our students have been the beneficiaries.

To our delight, The Lunch and Learn Series was recognized by the Ohio University administration at the April 2015 Leadership Awards Gala with an Outstanding Programming Award.[21]

Audrey Rule (State University of New York (SUNY) at Oswego), examined a content analysis of 45 journal articles that faculty members in the School of Education at SUNY-Oswego submitted as examples of authentic learning in their disciplines. Her summary uncovered four repeatedly found components, suggesting, as Rule writes, "They are an integral part of authentic learning experiences."

Those four descriptions of authentic learning are:

1. An activity that involves real-world problems and that mimics the work of professionals; the activity involves presentation of findings to audiences beyond the classroom.
2. Use of open-ended inquiry, thinking skills and metacognition.
3. Students engage in discourse and social learning in a community of learners.
4. Students direct their own learning in project work. [22]

These descriptions have guided the evolution of the Lunch and Learn Series. Additionally, our focus has unfailingly been to assure our students are attuned to the development of the soft character skills needed for success in authentic settings. The development of grit with the qualities of a growth mindset is interwoven in everything we do.

21 https://www.ohio.edu/compass/stories/14-15/4/2015-leadership-awards-gala-coverage.cfm
22 Rule, A. C., Arthur, S. C., Dunham, E., Miller, R., Stoker, J., Thibado, N. Preservice Elementary Teachers' Reflective Insights from Teaching Mathematics during an Authentic Early Practicum Experience. Journal of Authentic Learning, Volume 4, Number 1, Pages 43–64, June 2007.

ACKNOWLEDGEMENTS

This book originated as a collection of discernment questions that Paul Young began asking his students at the beginning of each lecture in his Introduction to Teacher Education Class (EDTE 1500). He immediately saw improvement in his students' commitment to learning and growing, and he shared his excitement with anyone who would listen. Two colleagues who heeded his suggestions and quickly began integrating discussions about grit and mindset in their classes were Terri Green and Debra Dunning. The result of many subsequent discussions has become an on-going collaboration that produced this book.

Collectively, we want to express our sincerest gratitude to Jim Grant, Executive Director of Staff Development for Educators, for his encouragement and constructive feedback pertaining to the original draft of the book. We also thank him for inspiring us, as well as our students, during presentations at our campus and for leading a courageous national campaign to help educators understand grit and mindset concepts and the need to develop grittier students in our schools.

Our colleagues at Ohio University have listened to our trials and tribulations but also celebrated our success. We also appreciate the encouragement, recognition, and praise for this work from our colleagues in the Gladys W. and David H. Patton College of Education at Ohio University in Athens.

Numerous area educators have shared their passion for working with children during our weekly Lunch and Learn Seminars. We are forever indebted for the time they willingly devote to helping us prepare high-quality teachers.

William England and the staff at Sentia Publishing expertly helped make our thoughts more concise, coherent, and compelling. They clearly understood the goals of this book and the needs of aspiring educators, and they knew how to develop a product that would meet those demands.

Most importantly, we appreciate our students—past, present, and future—who motivate us to work hard, think creatively, and respond in ways that none of us thought we ever could. They make us grittier and hold us accountable for modeling growth mindsets.

Lastly, we are blessed to have spouses, Gert Young, Mel Green, John Dunning, and families who provide continuous understanding of what teachers do, the time commitment that teaching requires, and the encouragement we all need. Their sacrifices have given us time to think, write, work together, share, and spread important messages with educators everywhere.

Paul Young, Terri Green, Debra Dunning
Lancaster, Ohio